Getting Transformation Right

A leader's guide to the management of change at scale

JANE LOGIE

Rᵉthink

First published in Great Britain in 2021
by Rethink Press (www.rethinkpress.com)

Contents

Introduction

Let's talk about the case for change. It's clear that the current pace of technological and digital advancement presents us with both an opportunity and a threat. Consumer behaviours are changing at a pace that would have been unimaginable even ten years ago. New entrants are disrupting our traditional marketplaces and creating new ways of doing business, so it's not a surprise that most organisations have some form of strategically driven transformation programme underway.

It's also no wonder that senior executives, having approved significant investment expenditure on the understanding that a programme will contribute to the continued success of their organisation, experience angst when that vital investment programme starts to show signs of failure.

If we accept that change is necessary to stay in the game these days, then we must also accept that the development of the skills and capabilities required to make this change part of the DNA of any future-focused organisation with big plans is simply a must.

My professional expertise has been gained over the last thirty years, including time spent in America developing global software for customer services, in Egypt creating a joint venture life insurance organisation and in the UK helping organisations to shape strategy, initiate, manage and turn around strategically focused portfolios and complex transformational programmes and projects.

Perhaps ironically, my single biggest failure when it comes to project management was in my personal life almost fifteen years ago when I decided to renovate a run-down yet charming eighteenth century Georgian house in the Welsh valleys. I didn't start out looking for a project. In fact, it was difficult to see how I could even consider taking one on as my work required me to spend most weekdays away from home, but I fell in love and convinced myself that I would be able to find a great builder to head up the renovation for me. I planned regular conference calls, reviewed plans online and checked progress in person at the weekends when at home.

This story is not a cautionary tale about my building company. In fact, they were perfect. They were patient and amenable, making endless decisions for me that I really should have been on site to make, and they eventually delivered a high-quality product which I am proud to call my home. What went wrong? I spent twice the budget that I had initially set aside, leaving myself in a position where for many years the only way that I could have sold my house would have been to sell at a loss.

I didn't intend to spend more than the local property market could stand. I had a plan that contained a set of core deliverables based on a set of ballpark costs.

As the project progressed though, there were literally a thousand decisions that had some impact on expenditure, and I often made these between meetings with little time to fully consider the cost implications. Decisions including should we spend an extra few hundred on hand-restoration of fireplaces? Should we level the bedroom floors, and did we really want a new freestanding tub in the bathroom (and the steels needed to support the weight)? Then there was the fixing of chimney pots, pointing the stonework, extra materials for the driveway and external lighting. The list was seemingly endless for the eighteen months that the project was in flight. As the cost estimates were replaced with actuals and as new work was added to the list, the 'cost to complete' number continued to increase and eventually ended up at double my original estimate.

I don't regret any of my decisions. I ended up with the home that I have always wanted. I also learned the best lesson about management of scope and costs possible. If I had been disciplined at the outset, I would have put more effort into getting the scope defined (what was out of scope, in particular). I would have used experts to inform my estimates rather than relying on Google and I would have been meticulous and budget focused. It's a good job I wasn't renovating the house to sell on at a profit because I would have failed stunningly.

As I have moved between organisations, I have seen repetitive underlying causes of failure occurring in large programmes and projects. This made me wonder, as a professional in the transformation field, how a discipline where learning should be baked into its general methodology can be so bad at identifying problems and learning from each other's mistakes. Combining my change and transformation knowledge with insight from fantastic colleagues that I have had the pleasure to work with over the years, I decided to consolidate some key learnings to get the ball rolling. I have organised this book into five main chapters. Chapter one focuses on ways of working that apply throughout the full transformation lifecycle. Chapters two through to five focus on specific capability areas. At the end of each chapter, I have included a checklist that can be used to guide and assess transformation performance.

It is my sincere hope that sharing these thoughts will provide readers with a better understanding of the common causes of failure, and those who are planning to embark on a complex transformation journey will be better able to avoid pitfalls and improve their chances of delivery success.

ONE

Ways Of Working

Jim Casey, the founder of United Parcel Service (UPS) used to say, 'There can be no glamour, no romance, no truly great success, unless shared in by all.'[1] Having spent ten years with UPS, this belief in the value of teamwork, combined with their ambitious plans and endless drive, has seen the organisation expand beyond its home in the USA into more than 220 countries and territories worldwide. I left UPS truly believing that a team that is outcome-focused, unified, that has a common way of describing its operations and ways of working and that holds each other to account is essential. I believe in the power of the team. A great

---

1   UPS, 'UPS Founders' Day: From teenage feet to global fleet', www.ups.com/us/en/services/resource-center/UPS-Founders-Day.page, accessed 25 May 2021

team will generally perform well regardless of the health of its underlying processes, whereas a team with poor behaviours will usually fail even if it has some of the best processes and tools in the world. This chapter explores the critical characteristics of high-performing transformation teams and the working methods that ensure their success.

Goal-focused

When thinking about the management of transformational change, I am reminded of the teachings of Stephen R Covey. In his book, *The 7 Habits of Highly Successful People*, habit two is to 'Begin with the end in mind.'[2] The ability to have a 'laser-like' focus on a compelling vision for the future while being as flexible and creative as possible when it comes to how things get done will deliver the right outcomes. Programmes and projects find themselves in difficulty when there is a general lack of understanding about what results or outcomes are truly important. Without a clear vision, the programme or project scope is likely to be vague. This makes it hard to plan properly and impossible to set and align team and individual objectives, which means that execution performance won't be great.

---

2   S Covey, *The 7 Habits of Highly Successful People: Powerful lessons in personal change* (First Press, 1989)

When it comes to the establishment of a new transformation programme, or when a transformation programme is setting up its constituent projects, attention must be paid to the definition, socialisation and approval of a vision, set of outcomes and/or objectives. Attention must also be paid to the ecosystem that the team inhabits and how it drives and focuses efforts on doing the right things consistently throughout the lifecycle. You need to make sure that the objective setting, performance appraisal system and contractor terms are driving the right outcomes and behaviours and focusing people on the most important goals.

Goal-focused teams:

- Have SMART (specific, measurable, achievable, realistic and timebound) objectives that link to the overarching programme goals, which in turn link to the business strategy. This level of alignment helps everyone to understand how they are personally contributing to the future success of the business (we all need to feel that we have an important role to play).

- Understand that the communication and tracking of progress is vital. Visual management tools and techniques make it possible to share information with others, communicate and enforce standards and bring attention to, react and prevent irregularities. There are some great tools available (including Kanban boards) designed to manage and improve the flow of work. These can be made available to all via collaboration tools like Trello (www.trello.com).

- Share their issues, identify challenges and work together to identify solutions. They have a 'we can do it' instead of an 'us versus them' attitude. They participate in lessons learned and retrospective sessions, understanding that sharing their experiences will help the wider team move forward in the future.

Thinking back to my home renovation, if the primary goal was selling my property at a profit as soon as it was finished, then every decision taken would have had to be made with these objectives in mind.

Team development

Transformation organisations are transitory in nature, made up of a complex matrix of both internal and external teams that can often be on- and offshore. This type of organisational complexity has a direct impact on the pace that teams move through the forming, storming, norming and performing stages of team development.

I commonly see supplier and/or inhouse teams at each other's throats, stuck in the forming or storming phases with little or no positive action being taken to resolve issues. The physical side of collaboration (eg, shared tools, agreed touch points and handoffs within process flows) and the roles that people play in the production of deliverables can be addressed through process design, training and on-the-job coaching. When issues arise, an approach that allows the team to quickly identify the underlying cause, co-create solutions and implement them fast is best for team development and programme delivery.

The softer side of team development also needs to be managed. The transitory structure means that pace is needed, but there are no shortcuts. A great way to kickstart team development is to focus on experiential learning by engaging new team members in immersive activities that mimic real life, allowing them to learn lessons with new colleagues by doing rather than listening. I love this type of intervention as it gives the participants a common experience, stories to tell and a shared language. Learning through this type of activity is real, collective and longer lasting. Twenty-five years ago, I attended my first experiential event called Gold of the Desert Kings, which was facilitated by Eagle's Flight (www.eaglesflight.com – look them up, they are fab). It made a real impact, and I've since organised experiences with numerous teams over the years, all of which have made a big difference to those involved.

Great teams that build strong foundations with a high degree of trust are speedy, they make decisions faster, they are high energy and are happier. In his book *The Speed of Trust*, Stephen Covey helps to unpack the importance of trust and how to build high-trust teams. It includes a supporting 360-degree survey that I recommend.[3] Unlike 'business as usual' teams, you often have consultants or contractors leading programme activities who are accountable for the delivery of work/product. Where there are permanent staff allocated to programme activities, they will usually have a line manager outside of the programme who is responsible for their pastoral care. Where this type of split exists, it's important that individuals are not given conflicting direction. The easiest way to avoid problems is for objectives to be drafted by the programme team and agreed with the line manager and for performance feedback to be provided when required.

Finally, it's really important that programme team members are generous with their expertise and are willing to share, coach and mentor less experienced members of their matrix team. If you have senior consulting or contract staff in leadership positions that don't see this as being part of their job, then replace them.

Common language

When I talk about a common language, I am specifically focusing on the use of terminology and how it is used

---

3   S Covey, *The Speed of Trust: The one thing that changes everything* (Simon & Schuster UK, 2008)

within a complex programme and project environment as a form of shorthand. If used properly it can lead to improved communication between team members and increased productivity. Anyone that has worked with me will know that when I work with programme teams, I am obsessed by the language being used. I repeatedly find inconsistencies between what person A says/means and what person B hears/understands. This is almost always because they are using some form of shorthand and not sharing the same definition. As an example, a quick Google search of a term such as 'minimum viable product' will produce a multitude of definitions which are often quite different. The same applies for other common portfolio, programme, project, workstream, architecture, analysis, development and test terminology.

The problems associated with ill-defined use of terminology are exacerbated within programmes as people relay information across matrix teams. I am reminded of the story about a military order that was sent by a series of radio relays, with each operator taking down the command sent by the previous station and then repeating it to the next station in the series. At the start the message was, 'Send reinforcements, we are going to advance' and by the time it reached the last station it had transformed into, 'Send three and fourpence, we are going to a dance'. A different order indeed. To avoid confusion, make sure that terms used are clearly defined. During interactions between teams, check that they are using common definitions. If you do feel the need to use a term such as 'minimum viable product' or similar, then make sure everyone understands what it means in the context of the specific delivery rather than generically.

The use of technical jargon or internal shorthand beyond the programme team is also to be avoided as it leads to confusion among stakeholders, who often have little understanding of its meaning. As someone who enjoys both the methodical and the technical side of my profession, I have learned over time to limit my use of terminology because I know that it won't make sense to people outside of my profession. I also encourage executives to seek clarity when they are presented with unintelligible communications.

Clear accountability

Large programmes often have multiple teams working on various parts of a solution at the same time, so a lack of clarity about who is responsible for the production of specific deliverables to a specific level of quality by a specific date is a recipe for failure. All too often I see teams with roles that are not clearly defined or that overlap unnecessarily, leading to confusion about who is accountable for what. This confusion leads to poor productivity, delays, cost overruns, and more importantly, unhappy team members. Nobody comes to work with the intention of missing deadlines or to shirk responsibility, we all want to add value in general. If teams are not performing, then ask yourself where the accountability matrix is failing. Better yet, talk to the team that is closest to the work. They will know what's wrong and may also know how to fix it.

Having a clear accountability matrix avoids roles being missed and stops people crowding around roles. After all, if every player in a football team played as a striker, then who would help keep the opposing players away from the goal posts? A great friend of mine who has many years of experience working with complex supplier landscapes introduced me to the RACI matrix. A RACI matrix is a chart that maps deliverables (this can include tasks). Each item listed captures:

- The person **R**esponsible for doing the work

- The person **A**ccountable as an owner for the work

- The people who need to be **C**onsulted

- The people who need to be **I**nformed

Having used a RACI matrix for years, I am convinced that the value isn't in using it to police accountability; it's in the conversations that take place between team members during its construction. In my experience, when a RACI is produced in collaboration with stakeholders, it has a much better chance of being adhered to.

Common process

All too often I see complicated and ineffective processes that are over-engineered, have multiple steps, deal with all sorts of special cases and exemptions and involve far too many people. I am sure that nobody comes into work thinking, 'Today I'll design a terrible process,' but over time processes get fiddled with by various well-meaning people who add and fix bits of the end-to-end flow, to accommodate change or to make part of the flow more effective for them. Without control, these minor changes can eventually lead to overlap, duplication and unnecessary complication. It reminds me of the child's game where a piece of paper is folded into three equal parts. The first child draws the head, then folds the paper over so that the next child can't see what's been drawn. The second child then draws the body and again folds the paper and hands it to the third to draw the legs. When the paper is unfolded, the result is always a Frankenstein's monster.

When transformation programmes are being set up, every process needs to be examined to ensure that it will be effective. The old, waterfall 'business as usual' process for project management is unlikely to be fit for purpose and should be replaced with a new, engineered process. When defining your governance and control processes, make sure that they are right-sized, removing unnecessary barriers to progress while keeping a sufficient grip on quality.

Most importantly, make sure that processes are shared by everyone in the matrix. There is no point having teams in IT operating with a software delivery life-cycle that is different to the approach used by the programme team. The use of different names for stages, different deliverables and governance methods leads to inefficiency, confusion and failure. Bring together experts from the functions that will be involved in the production of deliverables to create a single process flow with a common set of stages, deliverables and governance. When doing this, encourage everyone to be open to the adoption of new ways of working and involve the team that defines the new, unified process in both the rollout and in the embedding of new ways of working.

While you have skilled consulting or contract resources deployed, also take the opportunity to test new ways of working that may become part of your standard operating procedure longer-term.

Limit handoffs

In the context of transformation management, I am 'handoff' phobic. Handoffs (when a person passes infor-mation and execution to someone else in the delivera-ble production chain) create an opportunity for failure. While I accept that aiming for zero handoffs is extreme when there are a wide range of people and functions involved in the production of deliverables, I regularly see examples where common practice requires multiple approvals (eg, a business requirement approval that is within the lead subject matters area of expertise but requires a whole range of other approvals). Challenge programme teams and the wider organisation to simplify approvals. In terms of deliverables, get as much of the initial work done by a single person, then by a single team if necessary, and then by two teams if unavoidable. When a handoff is needed, ensure that the person passing on a partially completed deliverable and the person receiving the work to complete discuss what is required for an effective exchange.

It is worth taking time to map out programme level processes and to scrutinise them for steps that add no value or that create unnecessary handoffs. Once you have done this, ruthlessly remove the waste and any unnecessary approvals.

Look at your tools. There are some great collaboration software options in the world of programme and project management that make it possible for people to collaborate effectively to produce workflow management and performance data. For example, Smartsheet (www.smartsheet.com) enables hundreds of users to collaborate on plans. Tools like Jira (www.atlassian.com) underpin the flow of work from early requirement definition, through delivery, into test, and finally, into production. Tools help to ensure that people in the deliverable chain have the same information, which will reduce errors. Having a single source of truth for management information will also keep everyone honest.

Measure twice, cut once

When I was a child there was nothing better than being allowed to play in my dad's workshop. My dad was a carpenter by trade, and he always had lots of jobs on the go which I would 'help' with. When he was about to cut a piece of wood, he would make a mark on it in pencil. This would be the saw line. Before he'd put the saw to the wood, he would always pull out the tape measure again and recheck the length, saying, 'Measure twice and cut once.' In my father's profession, double-checking measurements for accuracy before sawing into a plank was essential as getting it wrong would mean that another piece of wood would need to be cut, doubling up on the time and materials used.

The same principle applies with programmes, especially at the outset where it pays dividends to spend time to get the setup right. If you don't have the expertise to set up a complex program with a complicated supplier landscape, don't try to do it unaided. At programme initiation, packaging up of work into deliverable chunks with a focus on the removal of dependencies and risks aligned with an appropriate methodology is essential, as is the need to build a structure that can deliver into a live environment early and often as large programmes with lengthy delivery lifecycles often fail.

During the definition of requirements, a focus on quality will underpin solid design and development processes. Carrying out static testing of requirements as they are gathered identifies defects and allows changes to be made before a single line of code is cut. My own experience is that around half of the defects found during testing could have usually been picked up during static testing if it had been considered important.

If applied throughout the lifecycle of any programme, the ways of working discussed above will underpin success. If you have teams who are outcome- and quality-focused, are unified behind a team purpose, are using the same language underpinned by a clear set of accountabilities and pragmatic, shared processes with minimal handoffs, they will be a force to reckon with.

Executive engagement

In the same way that building common processes and ways of working within the programme team is essential, it is vital that stakeholders within the wider community are engaged properly. Successful transformation programmes have an executive board who define the vision for change and are involved in the provision of oversight and sponsorship. Project level sponsors are drawn from areas of the business that have the most to gain or that will feel the most pain, that have the desire to lead change and the time to engage fully in the shaping of deliverables.

DISENGAGED EXECUTIVES

As an example of how poor stakeholder engagement can have a negative impact on programmes, I am reminded of an organisation that I worked with some time ago conducting assurance activities. As part of the early diagnostic conversations with the executive team, it quickly became clear that the company had a track record of large changes being driven by the centre, with leaders at the coalface feeling as though the changes were being foisted upon them rather than them feeling engaged and able to influence the solution.

People talked about how business changes delivered had broken processes and caused inefficiency and customer harm. Management felt like they were genuinely in a 'no win' situation with their teams who questioned why they had not done more to protect them from an unsuitable solution, and the centre (who criticised them for their lack of support). The management team were eventually listened to but far too late in the process, having initially been told to 'just do it', which failed horribly.

When considering engagement and sponsorship, think about the executive team. Which members will feel the greatest pain during implementation, and which will eventually reap the largest benefit? As an example, the implementation of Salesforce software will inevitably lead to pain for sales as they roll out the new technology and upskill their people, but when the benefits of great relationship management (increased conversion rates/sales) start to flow through, the initial upskilling challenge will soon be forgotten.

Where possible, I like to create a sponsorship model for transformation programmes. Each member of the executive team is accountable for an initiative, meaning that they lead the effort on behalf of the wider group, but need their peers to work with them to deliver the eventual benefits. This type of model means that the executive team need each other to be successful. It drives positive teamwork and helps to remove risks associated with personal agendas distracting from the core.

CONFLICTING AGENDAS

At one company I worked with, the eight executives on the board each had individual objectives linked to their specific roles that were directly linked to the executive reward scheme. The Chief Marketing Officer (CMO) had targets which were generally focused on new business volume growth, and the Chief Operating Officer (COO) on the maintenance of service standards and reduction of operational costs. There was little incentive for the COO to support revenue-generating changes sponsored by the CMO: the initiatives to increase business volume would generate a need for more people and equipment, driving up absolute costs, and if resource levels were not increased to accommodate new volume, then there was the potential for service backlogs and failures.

During the annual investment bidding process, the CMO and COO were both busy building a coalition of support for their individual investment proposals, as were the other six members of the executive team (who, in a similar manner, had their own specific objectives and pet projects). The bun fight that ensued was at times bloody and unproductive, with benefits being overstated and costs understated to improve their appeal. The final outcome of the investment bidding war was that to keep everyone happy, everyone got part of their investment funding, but nobody won the amount required. As a result, every project started out somewhat underfunded, with compromises being made everywhere.

During the delivery cycle, the 'personal agenda behaviour' continued, especially when there was contention between teams for scarce resources. The behaviour of the executives was modelled elsewhere in the organisation, driving aberrant behaviours in teams, and employee engagement scores were poor. Verbatim comments clearly indicated that the perceived in-fighting and lack of a common and shared agenda was driving confusion. I am sure that you won't be surprised to hear that delivery performance was measured through adherence to schedule and cost, and quality was atrocious.

This is a good example of how bad investment portfolio management can create an environment that drives the wrong behaviours. Having a clear set of shared objectives for the executive team will make a difference. Had the CMO and COO both been accountable for increasing new business as well as managing the cost of service, they would have been more likely to work together to identify low-cost, good quality streams of new revenue. When it comes to transformation, in addition to doing a few high-impact things well, having an executive team that win or lose together is essential. We need everyone at the top table asking what they can do to help rather than focusing on individual agendas.

Build in quality

We know that projects are more likely to be a success when the end users, subject matter experts and project team members work together in a collaborative manner from the start of the project through to its eventual closure. When this happens, the requirements defined are more likely to be fit for purpose and the solution eventually delivered better able to deliver the required business benefits.

In most organisations, what happens in practice is that users are engaged via the business analysis function during the requirements definition stage by attending workshops and reviewing outputs. Once requirements are signed off and during the design and build stage, they may occasionally be called upon to answer specific, business-related questions, but generally they are treated as passive bystanders until the project is ready for user acceptance testing. When the project is finally ready for the user to see what has been delivered, to their shock and horror, they find that their needs have been lost in translation between the analysts and developers or in the great prioritisation debate that rages during the lifecycle of any project.

The implications of poor collaboration with the end user community are far-reaching and painful. When they are not engineered to handle change well, costs increase exponentially when projects attempt to accommodate change to requirements during later phases of delivery. There is no doubt that the earlier an issue is found with a requirement, the lower the cost of resolution. For example, if you find an error during the requirements gathering and analysis stage, it is usually quick to fix with a minor correction made to the requirements specification artefacts. In the same way, when an issue is found in the design stage, the design artefacts can be corrected and re-issued. If the issue is not caught in the requirements and design phases, then the cost to fix it will be exponentially higher because we are not just talking about changing artefacts at this point; we are talking about making changes to code that has been developed and tested with all the resulting overheads.

As a professional community the implications of late identification of issues with requirements is well understood, and there should be a real drive to place more attention on improving the quality of deliverables during the early stages of the delivery lifecycle. This is known as shifting left. Your test management team should be given the opportunity to discuss the importance of shifting left. I would be surprised if members weren't exhilarated by the prospect of having your support for a focus on quality at the point of the production of analysis deliverables.

While the test community is likely to be supportive of the need to shift left, you may want to check with your test management team that it has the resources available to shift left both in terms of capacity and capability. If this is a yes, then lend the team members your support and accept the additional upfront costs as it will save a fortune. If they don't have the capability or capacity, then ask them to build it. A shift left also requires the analysis community to change the way that they work. They will need to get used to engaging with the test teams during the requirements elicitation stage and to receive and act upon feedback.

Analysis paralysis

A common issue is projects getting stuck in the requirements definition stage. This usually happens when insufficient thought has gone into the requirements definition approach. Unless processes and practices are tightly controlled, organisations can develop different ways of working within their various business units. One organisation I spent time with had ten business units each operating a different set of processes despite them having the same customer profile and product set. If the transformation programme had set out to define a set of business requirements for this organisation with all of its accepted differences, it would have ended up with somewhere between 30–50% more requirements and a business rules catalogue that was almost twice the necessary size. The extra requirements and rules would have made the delivery far more complex than it needed to be and costs would have been substantially higher. If your organisation sounds similar to the one above, then before you start your requirements definition phase, you need to bring your subject matter expert community together for each process to consolidate and unify around a new, common process. This will save both time and money.

Another common reason for projects failing to progress with pace through the requirements definition stage is fear. If an organisation has a culture where people are afraid of failure then the desire by business analysts, subject matter experts and the wider community to agree everything by committee to avoid personal risk should be expected. If fear exists, then expect to see:

- Lengthy, unproductive meetings

- Lots of opinions being expressed, but no decisions made

- More information being sought

- Requirements getting signed off, but with lots of caveats

- Nobody feeling accountable

- Everyone feeling able to throw rocks at what's delivered

If this sounds like your organisation, then there is a steep hill to climb before being able to successfully drive a complex transformation. Getting the foundation right and redesigning business processes upfront with the aim of simplification and standardisation is essential, as is the focus on quality during the requirements definition stage.

I usually advise organisations to consider the use of product owners if they have the opportunity. A product owner is typically a subject matter expert who is well respected by the wider business community, who understands exactly what the specific initiative is aiming to deliver and is able to make decisions on behalf of their colleagues. Product owners help with the definition of business requirements, prioritise work for the development teams and help the development and test teams to understand what is needed. They effectively bridge the gap between the business and various technical disciplines. If you are able to fully empower a single, trusted person and willing to offer your unconditional support, then the likelihood of successful delivery with a solution that users can really cheer about is more likely.

Bear in mind that being assigned to a critical programme or project as a subject matter expert, key user or product owner takes time. It's a bit like being a sponsor; it can't be done off the side of your desk. As part of normal estimation, the programme and/or project managers should assess the effort required from business subject matter experts well in advance of the need arising. This will allow arrangements to be made to handle 'business as usual' work. If you don't have sufficient capacity to enable your business subject matter experts to engage fully then don't progress as this will waste time and money and result in failure.

Cost management

A major part of programme and project management is the upfront and ongoing estimation, tracking and reporting of costs. This is often where problems with programme performance become evident. You may have observed a situation where a long-suffering programme sponsor (often armed with what can only be described as poor excuses) is facing an unhappy board of directors for the third time to seek funding approval for yet another costly overspend.

There is a great deal of research available that looks at the percentage of programmes that overspend over time and the costs associated with these failures. Research by the Association of Project Management found that nearly 80% of projects fail to wholly meet their planned objectives.[4] The reality is that we often don't need to look much beyond our own organisational

---

4   Association of Project Management, 'Conditions for Project Success: APM research report' (APM.org.uk, no date), www.apm.org.uk/media/1621/conditions-for-project-success_web_final_0.pdf, accessed 22 April 2021

boundaries or our wider peer network to find numerous examples of programmes that have failed to meet cost and other expectations. Whenever I work with a new client, I ask for copies of audit reports from historic programmes that have struggled. These reveal a lot about the common themes that have underpinned failure within that specific organisation, and I can then plan to avoid the same pitfalls.

If you experience cost overruns frequently, then the underlying estimation approach may be poor and/or the process for the management of financials may not be fit for purpose.

INACCURATE BUDGETING

I was associated with a financial organisation some years ago that had an investment portfolio of somewhere between £150m and £200m per annum. The organisation was focused on the management of programmes and projects against their approved budgets, but they had little success as each year a significant number of initiatives ended up in financial difficulty.

Assessment of the underlying reasons for the discrepancies between the approved budget and actual costs were analysed, with a number of key themes appearing. Key areas of concern included poor portfolio management practices, estimation difficulties (including optimism bias), mishandling of uncertainty, failure to maintain estimation discipline throughout the lifecycle, contractual difficulties and scope-related considerations. Once highlighted, the organisation was able to progress with a series of interventions that eventually had a positive impact on their cost management performance, one of which was to regularly evaluate the underlying causes of failure.

Portfolio management

The investment management lifecycle within any organisation has a massive part to play in how programmes operate. A colleague worked with a large insurance organisation where the board made a decision to fund an annual investment portfolio that was a whopping 30% larger than usual with no obvious regard to the do-ability beyond financial considerations. A whole range of initiatives were granted funding and sponsors were lined up to hit the ground running at the start of the financial year. They ended up jostling with each other for position and constrained resources and were all less productive as a result.

Good portfolio management not only challenges the organisation to evaluate investments, but also to spend money on the things that will add most value and to aid the understanding of resource and other constraints. I regularly ask boards to make difficult decisions about the merits of initiative A over initiative B and where to then draw the line in terms of total spend and associated resources. Where the right decision support is in place, a position is arrived at where a business portfolio is optimised to deliver maximum benefit that is sufficiently funded and do-able from a resource perspective. In summary, my philosophy is, 'Don't start what you can't finish.' Pick your programmes and projects. Do not run your portfolio like a horse race with everyone leaving the stalls at the same time; organise them in an optimised manner.

Estimation

An estimate is a calculation of the value, number, quantity or extent of something. In programme management this is usually the costs of buildings, facilities, hardware, software and all types of costed effort. An estimate is not the actual cost of something. It is flexible and based on the best information available at a given point in time. Transformation programmes generally approach estimation top down at outset, calculating what level of investment is affordable over a specific time period to achieve a set of desired business outcomes. Once the programme is in flight then estimates are more likely to be bottom up, with constituent projects producing estimates for both costs and benefits and these being amalgamated with programme level overheads to arrive at a total cost and benefit picture.

Not all programme directors or project managers are equal when it comes to estimation. I know many experienced professionals who are great at turning the handle on programmes and projects once they have been set up with a good plan and an associated budget but are totally incapable of starting from a blank piece of paper. If you do not have inhouse experience, then you may want to consider bringing in an experienced transformation specialist who will be able to work with your less experienced team members in the production of a more well-considered set of estimates. If your organisation has implemented similar solutions elsewhere within the group then make sure you encourage professional collaboration, as your colleagues are bound to have valuable insights to share. Lastly, take time to personally evaluate and examine estimates produced, checking for evidence and validating the programme team's thinking on assumptions and risks.

The knock-on impacts of poor estimating can be significant. In most organisations there is a set amount that can be invested annually, with change initiatives vying on an annual basis for their share of investment cash. If the board carve out cash for a programme which has understated its costs, then the organisation can find itself in a difficult position when an overspend arises. Where this happens, and if the options to avoid an overspend have been fully explored and there is no way to avoid it, then there are three common responses:

1. Delay expenditure within the year and allocate spend in the subsequent year. This option usually involves slowing down of expenditure. While this

can appear attractive, it is often associated with a ramp down and eventual ramp up in resource levels, which can be particularly difficult when working with third party suppliers. This type of ramp up and down approach is frequently slow to implement and often impacts long term productivity. This option can often cost more than the other two.

2. Continue and overspend against the investment budget. This may have a direct impact on profitability, which may or may not be acceptable.

3. Continue and terminate, or slow down, another initiative in the investment portfolio to free up the additional funding required. This is often the option chosen and can be useful at the start of a financial period where initiatives have yet to spend substantial percentages of their associated investment. Later in the financial year when substantial investment has been made in most initiatives, the sunk costs and the loss of the eventual benefit associated with the delayed or removed initiative can make this option far from attractive.

Regardless of the option selected, poor estimation undermines good investment portfolio planning and management and leads to programme and project level failure. Estimation isn't easy, but it's essential. Time spent getting estimates right will underpin good decision making at the portfolio, programme and project level. Effective estimation in conjunction with great portfolio management disciplines will reduce the risk of overspending against your investment budget and avoid funds being allocated where they are not required. Scrutinise estimates produced and look for regular updates as more information becomes available. Seek input regarding how ranges have been arrived at and what needs to be true in order for estimation ranges to be narrowed.

Adjusting for uncertainty

Does your organisation have a policy that drives the production of the business case early in the change lifecycle? At the start of a transformation programme, you have a high-level vision that is linked to your strategic goals, but you know almost nothing about the end products, so it is usual for ballpark estimates produced in the early stage to be associated with a high degree of uncertainty. As you do more work to define your transformation scope and its constituent projects, this uncertainty reduces. Once projects have defined their requirements and completed their designs and these designs have been integrated into the business and technology architecture blueprints at programme level, your position is much improved. When you get round to the selection of your suppliers then your position changes again, with costs being formalised as part of delivery contracts and statements of work. When you eventually start to deliver and see projects producing and implementing features, you are on the home straight.

Uncertainty after this point reduces as you deliver more, ending at 0% where everything has been delivered.

When considering budgets for transformation programmes, this progression from early ballpark estimates with low confidence through to definitive estimates with high confidence is super important. The *Software Project Survival Guide* was the first to coin the term 'cone of uncertainty' to describe this concept.[5] When we see a transformation programme come back for more money time and again it is probably because the number at outset was underpinned by rough order of magnitude (ROM) and unrealistic costs. Programme teams can also set themselves up to fail by making firm commitments too early in the lifecycle, especially when sponsors have a number in mind. As a sponsor of a transformation programme, my advice to you in the early stages of delivery is to seek a range from your team and expect this range to be wide. If you are not willing to fund at the top end of the range, then you may need to rethink the investment.

The worst case that I have seen is a programme which was focused on responding to a significant change in regulation in the financial services sector. It had produced a business case well before the scope was understood, using a set of magical pinpoint estimates. These had then been baked into the business case with zero contingency at programme level to address unforeseen

---

5   S McConnell, *Software Project Survival Guide* (Microsoft Press, 1997)

costs. The programme failed from a financial perspective, which was no surprise. For it have done anything else would have been a coincidence.

It's important to remember that sponsors are responsible for providing the resources to a programme, including cash. They need make sure that estimation models used to underpin programmes or projects are robust and that the teams involved are ready to review estimated costs at each stage in the lifecycle, taking into account the prevailing status of the initiative and the latest information available.

FLYING BLIND

A colleague was charged with turning around a programme that was in serious difficulty. It soon became obvious that the programme had produced estimates associated with a broad range, but the sponsor had only elected to share the low-end costs with the board. Based on these numbers, the board supported the programme, but as it initiated its constituent projects and they in turn contributed their estimates to programme level costs, the initial investment number was quickly exceeded.

At this point the sponsor was in difficulty with a programme that was in its early stages and already underfunded. The board, worried that the programme which was central to the achievement of strategic growth goals would not deliver, parted ways with the executive sponsor. Expert resources were brought in to re-initiate the programme, which continued on a revised, more secure basis. It eventually delivered the required benefits within planned budget and timescales.

If a programme is really worth doing, then using a range won't put the board off; in fact, it underpins better decision making.

Another common underlying issue observed when it comes to estimation of programme costs is a failure to cost the integration between software components. I have carried out assurance on a number of programmes over the last ten years where the business case understated costs as a result of missing interface/integration costs. This specific issue underpins the need to have a capable technical architect as part of the programme leadership team, which I will discuss in due course.

Cost increases

Cost overruns, which I will define here as 'spending more cash to get nothing more than we originally wanted and signed up to' are bad, but there can be valid reasons for spending more. For example, Solvency 2 regulations which set out requirements for insurance firms and groups covering financial resources, governance and accountability, risk assessment and management, supervisor, reporting and public disclosure were implemented on the 1 January 2016.[6] Responding to the Solvency 2 challenge, financial institutions had no choice but to initiate programme activities based on high-level directional information.

EYES WIDE OPEN

A colleague who was heading up a Solvency 2 programme at the time estimated costs based on a high-level set of assumptions and allowed for a contingency for unknowns of 40%, with budgets being agreed on the understanding that there was a high degree of uncertainty due to 'known' gaps in information. During the definition stage of the programme, the government legislation was developed, and more granular information became available. As expected, underlying high-level assumptions proved to be invalid. The associated estimates were subsequently found to be understated and the use of contingency could not address the funding gap. At this point, in consultation with the sponsor, the programme took a step back and carried out a bottom-up review of estimates based on more complete information, considered the scope and identified lower priority requirements that could be dropped. They eventually arrived at a revised set of costs which were approved by the board and that funded the delivery of the full solution into production within desired timescales.

---

6   Legislation.gov.uk, 'The Solvency 2 Regulations 2015' (Legislation. gov.uk), www.legislation.gov.uk/uksi/2015/575/contents, accessed 21 April 2021

In the example above, all the information required was simply not available to arrive at a confident estimate early in the programme lifecycle. In this case the sponsor, programme team and key stakeholders understood that the funding being sought was based on a low confidence estimate and that there was potential for a high degree of variation. Change is inevitable and not all additional funding requests are bad, especially when we enter into any funding arrangement with a full understanding of underlying estimation confidence and where additional funding leads to attractive additional benefits.

INCREASING YIELD

A programme focused on digital enablement for a personal loans business found during the customer research phase that by giving the client more ways to make repayments, conversion rates from quote to sale were substantially higher. Having carried out a full impact assessment, the programme was sure that the additional scope could be accommodated without suffering a negative impact on overall delivery performance and having evaluated the cost of offering the additional payment options and the increased purchase rates, a formal change request was approved based on the improved return on investment.

Inflated claims

Estimates that are not precise are associated with varying degrees of uncertainty depending on the stage that the work is in, the programme or project lifecycle and the information available. With this in mind, it would seem unlikely that anyone would be able to hit the nail on the head every time. If you have a track record within your organisation of programme and projects coming in regularly under budget, then you may have a different, yet equally worrying, problem.

I have seen organisations that, as a result of painful experiences with large programme failure and cost overruns, have adopted behaviours which make programme and project teams fearful of perceived failure. If a programme or project manager is punished for overspends and rewarded for coming in under budget then there is a clear incentive to inflate estimates, build in additional contingency and add in risk premiums, essentially overstating total costs to build a buffer large enough to cover almost any eventuality.

An organisation that I am familiar with implemented a performance management scheme based on the achievement of a number of project key performance indicators (KPIs), one of which was coming in under budget. Over the course of twenty-four months the number of projects coming in under budget increased dramatically, which was a positive change on the surface. However, at the portfolio level, fewer projects were being approved because projects were taking more than their fair and required share of the wider investment pot. Another example of bad measurement driving aberrant behaviour in an operational context goes back to the late 1990s where a call centre manager had set a target of 120 seconds per call for customer service representatives. Calls often took much longer than two minutes, so to achieve their targets agents started to answer and immediately hang up on callers to artificially lower their average call time. The saying 'you get what you measure' springs to mind. Where costs get overstated, initiatives will be awarded more cash than required, leaving other initiatives that could have delivered significant additional benefit sitting on the table.

Benefit management

How many of you can point to a programme or project that has delivered benefits exactly in line with business case estimates? If you can, then you are doing well. In its 2020 report on project management, Wellingtone states that just 40% of organisations say that they mostly or always deliver full project benefits.[7]

---

7   V Hines, 'The State Of Project Management Report 2020' (Wellingtone, 2020), https://wellingtone.co.uk/wp-content /uploads/2020/06/The-State-of-Project-Management-Report-2020 -Wellingtone.pdf

A clever actuary at a large insurance organisation worked out that margin could be improved by increasing the number of decimal places used in premium calculations. A project was set up to implement a technical change that had no user impact and delivered the benefits as soon as it went live. The improved profit position enabled the company to fund the launch of a new, market-winning pricing strategy. Wouldn't it be great if all programmes and projects were able to deliver their benefits at the point of implementation?

Unfortunately, what frequently happens is that benefits that have been committed to as part of the business case seem to mysteriously disappear, for example, that Customer Relationship Management system implementation that was planned to cost £1.5m and deliver increased annual sales of £6m but couldn't point to one additional sale, or the process automation project that introduced all sorts of new ways of working (and perhaps even some robotics), but had little or no real impact on either process efficiency, operational costs or customer experience.

I suspect that there are a lot of jaded boards out there that, when presented with a business case setting out a ten-fold financial return on investment pitches, see it as just another attractive, yet unrealistic, pipedream.

These are some of the most common reasons that investments fail to deliver the level of benefits committed to:

- **Resistance:** Failure to put the programme infrastructure in place to underpin great change management will result in problems when it comes to embedding change. Expecting resistance to change and planning how to deal with it from the start will allow you to overcome objections.

- **Unrealisable:** A common unrealisable benefit is headcount savings linked to productivity increases. If you take a team of ten full-time people who are working and you automate part of the process, making the team 5% more efficient, this improvement may result in additional capacity, but it doesn't deliver cost savings as you can't remove half a person from the team.

- **Overstated:** Overstatement at the outset – perhaps to make a business case appear more attractive. When making an assessment of eventual benefits it is common for assumptions to be used which may or may not be valid. In the early stages of a programme or project a benefit estimate is likely to be at the ROM level, with derived numbers based on a set of assumptions usually producing a range (a guess). If you are a programme or project sponsor then you own the benefits case and the underlying assumptions, and you have to be confident that financials are robust when proposing your business case for approval. As an approver you should review proposed benefits with a critical eye and be prepared to challenge assumptions.

There are a number of ways to mitigate risk when considering new product investments. You could run focus groups with potential customers to validate your thinking about the product. If you want more robust insight, you could run a small-scale trail to test assumptions about the target market, product features and pricing. If benefits are related to productivity improvements, you can compare the difference between the 'as is' and 'to be' processes, identifying where productivity improvements occur and then test the identified areas with the product owner or the wider user community.

- **Lack of focus:** Once work gets underway it is so easy for sponsors to get absorbed in day-to-day management, especially when there are governance meetings to attend, stakeholders to manage, risks and issues to mitigate and resolve, plans to review and decisions to be made. Staying focused on the delivery of benefits is paramount. Let the team deal with the day-to-day management of work and focus your efforts on the transformation programme and its purpose, bringing attention to the need to deliver benefits. As a sponsor, you are ultimately responsible for the business case and on the hook for the realisation of benefits. You may be the sole beneficiary or have a matrix of peers that you will need to work with to implement and then realise benefits, but whatever the setup, it is you and not the programme or project team that are accountable so you need to keep everyone focused on the eventual outcomes required.

- **Loss of traceability:** At the outset you clearly defined your benefits and you underpinned them with a solid set of assumptions. Then the programme got started and a thousand small decisions were made that eroded your benefits. What your programme was missing was a traceability approach, which would have linked your benefits to business requirements all the way through the definition, design and development stages and then into test and implementation. What traceability does in practice is to stop decisions being taken without reference to the associated benefit impacts.

If we consider a large software delivery, there may be hundreds of defects to be resolved at times. Traceability helps the team to understand which defects should be the highest priority (being linked directly to the most important benefits) and allows test teams to focus on coverage related to the most important requirements. As a sponsor, when you are presented with any scope-related decisions the question should always be, 'Can you define the impact on benefits?' If the information isn't available, then dig your heels in until you get it.

Some years ago, I worked with an organisation where the board approved business cases without setting future benefit realisation checkpoints as they were convinced that it was too difficult to track realisation post-implementation. As a result, sponsors were not held to account, business cases were generally poor quality and programme team behaviour was poor. The best approach is for benefits to be baked into future business plans. For example, if a business case states improved productivity and is associated with headcount reductions, then reduce the operational budgets by this amount. If it states increased revenue, then adjust the new business target accordingly. Whatever happens, hold the sponsor accountable and bring them back to the board to evidence delivery of benefits.

Summary checklist

Aim for a team that is:

- Outcome-focused: A team that is outcome-focused and unified, speaks with a common language and each member holds each other to account.

- Results oriented: Has the transformation programme set up its constituent projects with a clear statement of what 'good' looks like?

- Unified: Is it clear who is accountable for what in the programme and has attention been paid to team building?

Ensure your team has a:

- Common language: Is terminology acting as an effective form of shorthand within the programme? Is terminology avoided in broader stakeholder communications?

- Clear line of accountability: Does the programme have a clear accountability matrix in place that is fit for purpose and clearly sets out who is accountable and responsible for deliverables?

- Pragmatic, shared processes: Are programme processes engineered to be effective, are control processes right-sized and does everyone involved understand them?

- Minimal need for intervention: Have processes been engineered to remove unnecessary handoffs and to ruthlessly remove unnecessary layers and approvals? Does the programme have appropriate collaboration tools?

Does your team have a:

- Tailored approach: At programme initiation, was work packaged into deliverable chunks with a focus on removal of dependencies and were a range of methodologies used to suit the characteristics of the work?

- Solid stakeholder landscape: Are the executive team personally invested and impacted by the changes? Are they able to make time available to sponsor the changes?

- Collaborative approach: Are end users, subject matter experts (SMEs) and project team members working together in a collaborative manner? Are the analyst community working collaboratively with the test function sufficiently early on in the process to identify issues with requirements?

- Requirements approach: Has the programme clearly defined its approach to the definition of requirements and considered the need for process consolidation and simplification?

- Healthy attitude to risk: Is the organisation culture one where there is a high degree of trust and where risk taking is accepted?

- Respect for product ownership: Is the organisation willing to fully empower a single, trusted businessperson and offer them unconditional support? Has time been made available for sponsors, product owners and SMEs to participate fully?

- Estimation capability: Does the programme have the required estimation skills? Are estimates carried out at key stages, considering bias and uncertainty and are they critically evaluated for suitability?

- Portfolio management process: Does portfolio management challenge the organisation to evaluate investments and to spend money on the things that will add most value? Does it understand resource constraints and does it seek decisions based on comparable facts? Does it lead to a schedule to start work that is manageable?

- Control of inflated claims: Does the culture of the organisation drive behaviours that lead to production of over-inflated claims, both in terms of costs and benefits?

- Benefit management system: Are benefits realisable and accurately stated and is there sufficient focus within the wider programme on the outcome and benefits? Are decisions made taking into account the impact on benefits, not just costs?

TWO

Strategic Thinking

The development of the skills and capabilities required to make change an integral part of any future-focused organisation is a must. In this chapter we will consider the intersection between business and transformation strategy, portfolio planning, business and technical architecture and unpack some of the common causes of failure.

Business strategy

One of the first things on my must-see priority list when starting any engagement with an organisation is a copy of their current business strategy and a schedule that lists initiatives currently being funded as part of the change portfolio. This helps me to assess the degree of alignment between the strategy and the change portfolio. It is common to find misalignment between the two, for example, the formal strategy being about business growth and improved customer advocacy, and the portfolio being focused on meeting regulatory requirements or improving efficiency to drive out costs and generally keeping the lights on.

Having a clear understanding of what the business is setting out to achieve over the medium term, taking into consideration the marketplace, where the organisation wants to play and how they think they will win, is what I expect to see encapsulated in a business strategy. This allows strategic planning to take place. Strategy starts to get translated into action, perhaps in the form of high-level road maps and associated key performance measures aligned to agreed strategic outcomes that can be used to guide and encourage the right behaviours.

Let's assume you have a clear business strategy and a high-level road map that considers the sorts of initiatives required to deliver results and sets out what you want to achieve and by when. You can then start to optimise and align the portfolio to make the most progress towards your strategic goals. There may also be a specific transformation strategy which goes beyond the typical business and operational strategies and focuses on radical and impactful changes on people, process and technology. A transformation programme is usually aligned with this type of strategy, as they are complex and often the domain of transformation specialists.

FAUX TRANSFORMATION

Having spent a few days reviewing a large finance transformation programme, it became evident that there were some sizeable issues to be resolved, including how the organisation had piled on all sorts of inappropriate overheads associated with a large transformation.

The scope of the programme was focused on the delivery of three large projects with some limited dependencies that impacted various parts of the organisation in some way, but collectively, they were not transformational in nature. In this case, the organisation didn't need an expensive transformation organisation; all that was needed was some good old-fashioned programme and project management done well. Labelled as a global transformation, the programme was populated by some really big-hitting resources that were expensive and had some fancy ideas about their roles, but in reality, few of the people engaged were able to actually roll up their sleeves and get the real work done. This is what happens when we call something a global transformation programme rather than a portfolio, or perhaps a project.

If you already have a clear strategy and you are confident that the gap between where you are now and where you want to be in the future has a major impact on people, process and systems, then it is important for a transformation strategy to be developed. The strategy will clearly link the strategic goals of the organisation to a programme of work and an eventual vision that you can share with key stakeholders to build a coalition of support.

I am a massive advocate for the development of a transformation story, which is a short statement of how the organisation will look after the programme has implemented the required changes. I often write this retrospectively by picking a future date and reflecting on how performance over a number of years will have improved.

A simple example of a how a retrospective statement might read:

'Over the last three years, business revenue has grown by 20%. We have contributed an additional £8m in profit to the group, our customers now have 24/7 access and customer engagement scores have improved by 15%. Our colleagues are happy, with engagement scores hitting an all-time high of 97%. Our focus on business agility now allows us to deliver innovative ideas that benefit our customers, colleagues and corporate stakeholders within a ninety-day period.'

A transformation story like this reminds everyone during the programme lifecycle why the structure exists. It focuses the minds of everyone involved on the outcomes needed and acts as a consistent thread for communication. It can also be massively useful when considering programme scope; if a proposed change doesn't pass the 'how do I impact the story' test, it makes it easy to reject and move on.

Having a clear vision will help with change management. When talking to people about change, you need to help them envisage the future and to make the changes that will impact them less daunting. If you can paint a picture of a larger, more profitable business with fulfilling jobs, you will have a much easier sell.

Before discussing the need to be clear about what your organisation is setting out to achieve, it is worth talking about goals. In particular, how many goals is too many? There should be somewhere between five to seven weighty goals, with a preference for five. There is a difference between achieving things that are quite important and things that are 'wildly important'.[8] A great friend of mine says, 'PIGS (pretty important goals) are the enemy of WIGS (wildly important goals).' Adam Merrill, the co-author of *The 5 Choices: The Path to Extraordinary Productivity* says, 'In today's environment the key to true productivity is not to get more done

---

8   C McChesney, S Covey and J Huling, *The 4 Disciplines of Execution: Revised and updated: Achieving your wildly important goals* (Simon and Schuster UK, 2021)

but to get the right things done.'[9] When it comes to transforming an organisation, having a laser-like focus on doing the wildly important incredibly well will drive greater delivery focus and success.

Portfolio planning

A portfolio is a collection of programmes and projects which are addressed collectively and aligned with a set of governance structures and services which support the optimisation of return on investment and the prioritisation of desired strategic outcomes. Where portfolio management is done well, it is often aligned with corporate governance and has a greater focus on strategically aligned change, little or no duplication and high levels of confidence in portfolio plans and underpinning resource profiles.

Great portfolio management will ensure that the organisation says no to many things, clearing the decks for a transformation programme to be successful. In organisations that understand what it takes to bring about a step change at pace, pet projects, small change projects, low impact changes and, at times, other fairly significant projects and programmes get canned. In doing so, the leaders are not saying that these are unimportant, they are just saying that they are not as important as

---

9   K Kogon, et al, *The 5 Choices: The path to extraordinary productivity* (Simon & Schuster, 2016)

the achievement of their WIGS and that they want to remove the distraction from the organisation.

DITCH THE DETAIL

An organisation that I worked with some time ago had a 'change board' which met monthly to discuss its small change portfolio. There were thirty-plus people on the attendee list, including the full executive team. Long-winded reports in excess of eighty pages were printed in advance of each meeting and the meetings had a reputation for running on for hours, often mired in unproductive detail. The projects discussed were mainly small and discretionary in nature with low benefit levels. The time spent by the board and the other attendees, who were all busy people, could have been better spent supporting their struggling transformation programme.

In the context of portfolio management and the need to make way for the wildly important, I am often faced with an argument that it's impossible to stop projects that are driven by regulatory change or that the need to address compliance concerns cannot be considered discretionary. My response is always the same: of course they need to be progressed, but the focus must be on doing as little as possible. In other words, make sure that the project does not accept anything into scope that is not directly linked to meeting the legal obligation and that the sponsor understands that there is no room for a 'while the bonnet is open' attitude.

Behaviour where sponsors use regulatory projects to sneak in those product tweaks that couldn't pass the return-on-investment test as initiatives in their own right must stop.

Finally, as with faux transformation, avoid faux portfolio management. For example, a list of small changes to meet regulatory obligations (all of which will require a handful of days) does not need expensive portfolio management structures and processes. They can be managed as a simple regulatory backlog with a reduced level of governance.

Let's assume that you have developed your business strategy and after due consideration decided that it is sufficiently impactful on your people, processes and systems to be considered transformational. You have defined a specific vision for a transformation programme and considered the needs of the programme alongside the needs of other priority initiatives, arriving at a finalised portfolio of change that you understand, support fully and know is do-able in terms of funding and resource capacity.

The next challenge is to be a strategic leader with the ability to express a strategic vision in such a way as to motivate and persuade others to work towards achievement of that vision. Strategic leaders understand that people need structure, and they work to create this, making required resources available while consistently focusing on the end game. They are ambitious, objective, able to deal with ambiguity and with broad and complex issues, and able to see the bigger picture.

As part of the work to create a strategy that could be understood by all, a credit business that I worked with some time ago took the goals and route map for change and gave them to a design agency who created a fantastic picture that illustrated all of the key changes in a visually engaging way. The strategy visualisation was used at town-hall and other communication sessions and was displayed at their various locations worldwide. As progress was made, they were able to use the visualisation to illustrate what had been completed and what was still to be done. Without strategic leadership to create and sell a compelling vision and to drive towards the vision with passion and unwavering focus, complex programmes will struggle to do difficult things.

SINGING FROM THE SAME SONG SHEET

I was asked to evaluate an inflight transformation programme that was in serious difficulty and as part of the assurance review timetable I arranged to spend time on a one-to-one basis with various members of the executive leadership team.

Keen to understand what it would take for me to deliver a successful outcome in her opinion, during my first session with the chief executive I asked her what an eleven out of ten performance (better than excellent) might look like. After thinking for a minute, she said that seeing her executive team standing shoulder to shoulder in alignment behind proposed changes was at the top of her list. A lack of alignment at the executive team level was a historical problem and she wanted the team to be completely bought into the vision and planned changes moving forward by actively engaging with people across the organisation, reinforcing the case for change and providing the programme with hands-on support and guidance.

Interestingly, during similar sessions with members of her executive team, it became clear to me that she was quite right to be concerned. There was little buy-in in evidence for the proposed changes. It seemed that the organisation had embarked on a transformation journey without doing essential alignment groundwork at the executive team level. The inflight programme was seen as an IT programme focused on the implementation of a range of technology solutions rather than as a business programme delivering a set of critical business outcomes. As a result, the executive team beyond the CEO and the IT director found it difficult to see how such expensive and potentially disruptive changes could add value to their business units and they were reluctant to commit valuable time and resources to the programme.

It is important to note that the executive team were not change-averse. In fact, they were quite the opposite, they were keen to see change that they could support being progressed. Individually, each team member was committed to the organisation, proud of its achievements to date and wanted to be part of the team that would enable the business to improve upon its already successful track record. They wanted to play a role in the definition of the key goals for the organisation and the decision making about what types of changes and investments would be backed.

I cannot stress enough that if your transformation programme is not clearly linked to your business strategy and to goals that the executive team can collectively get behind, then it will struggle to get support and then to sustain it, especially when times get tough (which they always do with any large and complex programme of change).

Sponsorship

Sponsors are business leaders who play a key role in promoting, advocating and shaping programme and project work. A sponsor will ideally have the most to gain from the change and they may also feel the most pain during transition. They are accountable for the production of the business case and supporting analysis used to trigger a funding decision, for maintaining the validity of this during the lifecycle and for ensuring the realisation of the specified benefits.

There is no shortcut to becoming a great sponsor. It's like everything else in life: the more you practice, the better you get. If you have an aggressive change agenda and the executive team have little or no experience sponsoring change of a similar size and complexity, then action will need to be taken to mitigate performance risks. Poor sponsors focus on the wrong things and they have a disruptive and negative influence on any programme.

ACCENTUATE THE POSITIVE

A colleague recounts a tale of a senior executive who was totally blind to anything perceived as being negative. The executive consistently shut down discussions regarding complex risks and dependencies and refused to report the factual status of the programme to the board.

The programme manager, who had learned over time working alongside the sponsor that transparency was met with anger and ignorance, had learned to mirror the behaviour and had encouraged the wider programme team to accentuate the positive when producing status reports.

Behind all this positivity, the programme was in material difficulty with a wide range of significant risks that could not be mitigated, hundreds of issues that were not being managed, plans that were unrealistic, dependencies that had been missed, suppliers that were out of control and a programme team that were hiding their disillusionment.

For a long time, the board members were blissfully unaware of the underlying issues and the implications. Unaware of the real state of affairs, they were unable to manage their external stakeholder community and when the programme eventually failed it did so in a way that was public and difficult to manage. After two years and millions being invested, the programme was terminated with zero delivered.

Great sponsors are not half full or half empty. They deal with facts, look to realistic metrics to support their assessment of performance and demonstrate real integrity and courage. They know what questions to ask, and they have a willingness to listen, hear and understand what they are being told. If sponsors are transparent, fearless and open to discussing problems without obfuscation, then the collective brains of the organisation can go to work on the solution. When leadership is working effectively, projects and programmes don't deliver surprises at board meetings.

Experienced executives and senior managers may have a wealth of experience at the leadership level in disciplines such as finance, operations, marketing or sales, but it doesn't follow that they have the knowledge, skills or experience required to be great sponsors. When we have a medical problem, we might search Google for the symptoms, but we generally see a doctor for a diagnosis and to prescribe treatment. The same applies for sponsorship of large transformation; it's not for the untried, untested, unskilled or faint of heart.

What options are available to you if you are planning to start a large, complex transformation programme and know that there is a lack of sponsorship knowledge, skill and experience within your organisation?

Option one: Consider hiring in expertise. If you happen to have a vacant position at the executive level, you could consider recruiting talent into the organisation that has a demonstrable and strong track record of successful sponsorship. If you do decide to take this approach, then you may want to seek assistance from a trusted advisor who can help you to evaluate the candidates.

A great sponsor will:

- Need to have a full understanding of the role and its significance.

- Have a strategic mindset, the ability to take the long view, and to make connections between the business strategy and the programme vision and project for others.

- Be a strong leader in both line and matrix structures, able to drive a culture of collaboration and be skilled when it comes to engaging stakeholders and building support, especially with difficult groups.

- Have credibility and be accepted by the various stakeholder's groups as trustworthy and being the right fit for the role.

- Need to be able to give the role sufficient time and priority in their agenda and be willing to take personal ownership and accountability for their part of the wider programme.

- Need to be able to influence people towards a successful outcome at all levels in the organisation (this may be difficult if new to the organisation).

Option two: Fund some form of external coaching for your sponsor/s. Consider contracting with a consulting organisation to provide hands-on, executive level coaching for you and members of your team performing sponsorship roles during the lifecycle of the programme. Most consulting organisations will have services readily available and be keen to engage in this type of activity. Within transformation there are all sorts of methods, tools and terms which are a form of shorthand that can dramatically improve efficiency and reduce confusion, but beyond the professional community this shorthand can have the opposite effect. Any consulting organisation will be able to demystify and unpack the sort of information presented. They will be able to assess the project's position and offer insight into what questions to ask and the stance to take as a sponsor. Although a fan of this approach, I do have a word of caution. Watch out for problems being overstated as a way to encourage you or your sponsor to buy more significant interventions.

I have experience with a reputable organisation called CITI (www.citi.co.uk) who have assisted senior leadership teams and individual sponsors in focusing correctly on the sponsorship of change.

Option three: Seek support from a peer. This is probably one of my favourite options and involves you seeking out a well-respected peer who has successfully led an organisation through a transformation that is similar in nature to the programme planned for your business. They will understand what it takes to do the job well, they will have learned through trial and error what does and doesn't work and be able to offer you valuable advice and guidance. Another benefit of this type of support arrangement is that they are unlikely to use language that you won't understand. Having been a sponsor myself on numerous occasions, I wish that I had considered having a peer mentor myself. It would have saved me significant pain and helped me avoid many nights of lost sleep. You could take this one step further, and in addition to regular one-to-one review sessions, you could ask them to attend your transformation oversight board and significant programme stage gate transitions meetings to provide some independent oversight. If you pick the right person, I can almost guarantee that they will ask questions that will add value.

Option four: Select a consulting organisation to provide you with regular and independent assurance services which provide you with an evaluation of the status of the transformation programme and its constituent projects. If you are upfront with the programme about your lack of expertise and if you pick the right consulting partner who can work with and not against the programme team, then this can provide you with a solid safety net. As part of the service, I would expect the assurance partner to produce action plans to address deficiencies and for the implementation of these to be in agreement with the programme team and validated as part of future assurance activities.

There is a massive amount of material available that sets out what great sponsorship looks like. APMG international (apmg-international.com) has a specific course focused on programme and project sponsorship which aims to develop the full spectrum of skills needed to be an effective sponsor and is offered by various suppliers. Prosci (www.prosci.com) has a change management sponsor briefing course where executives can learn how to make active and visible executive sponsorship part of their change initiatives. The barriers to training of this type are never cost; it's always the lack of availability of the prospective trainees. If your sponsors are unable to carve out sufficient time for a training course before they start, then they are unlikely to be able to sponsor a critical project.

Another common area of failure is the relationship between the sponsor and the programme or project manager. I regularly talk to sponsors who are unhappy with some part of their programme or project manager's performance. Sponsorship is a job with clear accountabilities that requires knowledge, skill and experience to do well. When it is done brilliantly, there is an upfront conversation where the contract between the sponsor and the programme or project manager is crafted to set out how they will work together and a series of check-ins are planned where performance against the contract can be reviewed.

RESPECTIVE EXPECTATIONS

An experienced COO at a bank was on point for the sponsorship of a business-critical data migration project as a result of a merger between two organisations. He discussed the pressure to 'get it right first time' to avoid customer impacts (which may have resulted in a public relations issue) but felt like he was the last to hear about significant issues and risks, with new information often being presented in front of the wider transformation programme board. This left him unable to respond to questions raised, and open to personal criticism at times. When I spoke to the data migration project manager, she was able to evidence that her sponsor had been invited to attend regular review meetings but had either failed to attend or had sent a deputy in his place. Her sponsor had also been sent papers to review well in advance of governance boards. What became clear was that they had not taken time to discuss how they would work together as sponsor and project manager and their respective expectations of one another.

Another common issue that I see time and again is the transformation director operating like a strange pseudo-sponsor, usually due to an abdication of responsibility by real sponsors. I understand that there are times where every executive is super-busy and there may be some merit in them asking the transformation director to provide air cover for brief periods. However, it's important to note that people want to hear about changes that will impact them from colleagues who they trust and work with on a day-to-day basis (ie, their boss or boss's boss). You need to avoid inappropriate sponsorship arrangements that may drive a perception that the transformation programme is doing things *to* impacted teams rather than *with* them. Sponsorship is best when done by functional owners who are trusted by their teams.

Do your sponsors have sufficient time to do the job well? You can be a sponsor between meetings, but you can't be a great sponsor off the side of your desk. The programme will need regular input from the sponsor as well as key SMEs that represent the user community. The sponsor will also have a significant number of decisions to make and to do this well they will need to be fully up to speed on a wide range of matters. They will also need to represent the programme with various stakeholder communities and to be there for everyone when the going gets tough, which it inevitably does.

One of the biggest complaints I hear when talking to busy executives who have been involved in sponsorship roles is that they were expected to take on the accountabilities in addition to demanding day jobs. Large sponsorship roles are full-time, so plans will need to be made to create the capacity for a member of your top team to dedicate their time to your transformation programme projects. The best approach is to onboard some form of interim cover, allowing the candidate to fully commit to the work. The backfill could be from an external organisation or it could be seen as a development opportunity for a rising star.

Finally, not all sponsorship roles are equal. If the transformation programme has a complex internal and external stakeholder landscape, complicated interdependent streams of work, a large, multi-supplier resource model, rock hard constraints, significant dependencies and is somewhat inventive in nature, then a first-class sponsor with a great deal of relevant experience is essential.

Business architecture

Organisations are made up of various functions that communicate and collaborate to achieve business outcomes. They inevitably have an architecture that underpins the delivery of business outcomes. These may or may not be valued and may or may not have been documented. The architecture may have been somewhat engineered with a strategic focus or it may have just emerged over time as the organisation has solved problems and exploited opportunities.

When it comes to transformation, understanding the current business architecture (often called the 'as is' state) is important as it provides you with a way to illustrate the organisation in terms of its current capabilities and maturity levels and then to overlay proposed changes, producing a 'to be' state with targeted maturity levels. You can then see the gap between the position you are in today vs your end design and can assess the overall size and complexity of the change required.

Where the business architecture has emerged rather than developed through design, functional duplication and fragmentation of processes and value chains are more likely to be observed, so you want to lead with design when it comes to real transformational change. How many times have you come across a project that is looking to introduce a capability uplift in data management and you find that to create the new world order, you need to migrate and decommission multiple technologies offering similar services to the business? This is often the by-product of a lack of design thinking.

Hiring a highly skilled business architect is an investment in the definition of a more effective future business model. They will be able to work with members of the executive team to scope out a set of high-level initiatives that are considered essential to meet the strategic vision and assess their individual and collective impacts on the current business model. Using this information, the transformation programme sponsor, or oversight board, can make decisions about which initiatives they wish to support. The business architect will also work with the transformation programme director to assess the optimal delivery order and timescales, producing a series of transition states which illustrate how the business will transform over time.

The transition state models will underpin wider change management activities and provide the programme with a series of waypoints where progress towards the eventual business architecture can be validated. At the end of a transition state, it should be safe to pause or halt if other priorities arise.

The business architect will act as a trusted advisor to the transformation director and the executive. They will have a line into each of the projects within the programme and oversee scope and solution, ensuring that there is continued alignment with approved architecture. If problems are encountered with delivery and significant scope decisions are required, they will provide unbiased decision support to the sponsor. My advice to organisations embarking on substantial change is to ideally recruit someone into this role that will be with the organisation over the long term and that will have skin in the game. The degree of understanding required to do this job well for a business is such that short term commitments using contractors will usually not be as successful.

Technical architecture

Let's start at the beginning. Information technology is the discipline that focuses on planning, configuring, installing and running computer systems allowing data to be stored, manipulated and moved in a way that enables the objective of the business to be met.

Both business and technical architectures are defined to achieve a set of business outcomes often described in the business as the IT or transformation strategy. IT architecture focuses on both hardware and software and associated services, defining the information processing assets, the rules that govern them and the associated information.

As with business architecture, the current technical architecture may have been designed or it may have emerged over time, potentially leading to some form of duplication. A transformation programme is often seen as a way to modernise and simplify technical architecture and as a way to deliver better-value services to the organisation over the medium to long term. With this in mind, and taking into account the fact that large transformation programmes frequently involve the delivery of multiple technologies via a range of providers, having an experienced technical architect on the team at outset is critical.

Although it is usual for transformation leaders to have a strong background in the delivery of technology, it is the technical architect that serves as the chief technologist for the entire initiative. This individual is responsible for evaluating technologies and products (from a technical perspective), determining and enforcing standards, architecting the models to be used in the exchange of data among various components and almost everything else technology related.

The technical architect is the voice of authority for all technology and technology-related architecture matters. This is often linked into a central enterprise architecture function that defines broader policies and practices and ensures that businesses within a group of companies (where relevant) remain aligned with the wider technology strategy.

They will lead the efforts to select technology for evaluating the various solutions options, selecting the one that is best suited to the needs of the project, programme and the wider organisation. They will act as a trusted advisor to the transformation leadership and the executive, being able to build an understanding of deeply technical matters in a way that makes sense to a non-technical audience. They will generally have a line into each of the component projects within a programme of work and will oversee technical matters, ensuring continued alignment with defined and approved architecture.

What goes wrong if technical architecture is not engaged, and architecture is allowed to develop outside of governance? I have seen a duplication of solutions which have increased the cost of ownership, point-to-point integrations between systems which have increased the cost of maintenance (and when visualised, looked like someone had dropped a bowl of spaghetti on the paper), ancient software and solutions that were out of support and costing a fortune, parts for failing equipment having to be bought on eBay, shadow IT adding to the IT estate (increasing cost of ownership numbers all over the place), skills shortages for outdated solutions blocking change, difficulty managing data security and consumer privacy, and an overwhelming focus on keeping the lights on for the ancient mess rather than investing in innovation.

When technical architecture is engaged fully, the designs produced will underpin effective selection, development and integration across the programme. In addition, technical architecture will ensure that the programme's constituent projects remain aligned to the architectural vision. If you are about to start your transformation journey, make sure that you have a competent, business-focused IT architecture specialist in place.

Summary checklist

In aiming for a clear business strategy, ensure you have:

- Robust business and technical architectures: A clear strategy with a vision for transformation underpinned by robust business and technical architectures that are able to deliver the required business outcomes.

- Key strategic goals: Is there a clearly documented business strategy and are the contents of the approved change portfolio weighted towards delivery of key strategic goals?

- A definitive road map: Is there a clearly documented, strategic road map setting out the key delivery initiatives in some sort of desired sequence and timeframe?

- A transformation strategy: Is there a clearly defined transformation strategy and does it link the strategic goals of the organisation directly to the programme of work?

- Vision: Is there a clear picture (retrospective and/ or visual) of how the organisation will look after the programme has implemented the proposed changes and disbanded?

- PIGS not WIGS: Does the organisation have a laser-like focus on achieving a few large, wildly important and impactful goals incredibly well?

- Portfolio optimisation: Is your change portfolio optimised for return on investment and the prioritisation of desired strategic outcomes?

- Portfolio confidence: Are you confident that there is little or no duplication and overlap within your investment portfolio and is confidence underpinning resource schedules high?

- Positive change management: Are key leaders in the organisation able to express a strategic vision that motivates and persuades others to work towards the achievement of proposed changes?

- Alignment: Are the executive leadership team collectively bought into the strategy and the linked programme of work and are they singing off the same song sheet?

- Current state assessment: Is the 'as is' state defined and understood and does it illustrate the current level of maturity by capability area?

- Future state design and gap: Is the 'to be' state defined and is the gap between the 'as is' and 'to be' states at the capability level understood?

- Decision support: Has the executive been able to make decisions regarding initiatives that are to be part of the programme, taking into account the individual and collective ability of the organisation to deliver the required strategic outcomes?

- Transition states: Does the programme have a clear set of transition states defined which illustrate how the business will transform over time?

- Business architecture governance: Is business architecture overseeing the scope and solution ensuring that there is continued alignment with approved architecture?

- Programme technologist: Does the programme have a dedicated technical architect that serves as the chief technologist for the entire initiative?

- Technical evaluation: Is the technical architect responsible for evaluating technologies and products (from a technical perspective)?

- Technical architecture governance: Is the technical architect overseeing technical matters to ensure continued alignment with defined and approved architecture?

- Sponsors who:

  - Play a key role in promoting, advocating and shaping programme and project work?

  - Are accountable for ensuring the realisation of the specified benefits and for the production of the business case?

  - Deal in facts, looking to realistic metrics to support their assessment of performance and demonstrating real integrity and courage?

  - Know what questions to ask and do they have a willingness to listen, hear and understand what they are being told?

  - Have the knowledge, skill and experience to do the job well? If not, has action been taken to address gaps?

  - Have the time available in their busy days to do the job well?

  - Have a contract with the programme or project manager which sets out how they will work together?

– Have trust as functional owners, are trusted by their teams and have the most to gain and/or feel the most pain?

– Attend necessary meetings, keep up to date with progress, issues, risks and plans and provide prompt support to the programme or project team when required?

THREE

Setting Up For Success

Now that you are aware of the importance of getting the right ways of working in place and how these are essential if a large transformation programme is to be successful, I want to build on this foundation. This chapter will discuss how the scope of a programme can be broken down into deliverable chunks, how to best govern the work, how programme and project management, analysis and test management intersect to achieve a successful delivery outcome and the importance of having a solid vendor selection process.

Strategic thinking

In the previous chapter we focused on the development of planned business strategies and the creation of transformation programmes based on a formal process and driven by a specific strategy and associated objectives. The alternative to the planned genesis is where initiatives have emerged in a piecemeal fashion as the business has been forced to respond to events as they arise, for example, changes in the external environment such as regulations.

Emergent programmes are often less strategic in nature, but still vital. Regardless of the genesis, this stage in the process should not be avoided. This means that emergent programmes may need to pause and take a step backward to put the foundations required for future delivery success into place. If an emergent programme is already in trouble (having spent more and taken longer than desired) then it may be undesirable to take a pause but doing so will avoid spending more money on something that may already be fundamentally flawed. Why is it important to stop and take stock? Let's look at a real-life example.

TRAVELLING IN THE TRAJECTORY OF HOPE

A large service provider with a sizeable customer base decided to implement a software package that would enable them to optimise and automate the planning of service routes. They believed that the implementation would deliver improved efficiency, creating capacity for business growth. They selected a leading-edge software product and a partner to help them to design and configure the rules that would underpin the software's scheduling routines. After a period of configuration and testing of the software they implemented the solution across the UK within the originally specified timeframes. All good so far.

However, the configured rules proved to be immature, drivers became frustrated with routes that they were unable to follow and were impacting their bonus payments, and call centre complaint volumes went through the roof as a result of missed and late service visits. Despite the evidence that the situation was dire the organisation continued to build additional rules, essentially on the fly, hoping that complaints would start to drop off. They didn't.

Given the impact that the introduction of this new scheduling software had on internal functions such as distribution and the contact centre, and the real impact of poor service on the customers, the work could certainly have been packaged differently to reduce risk. For example, the project could have started out with a proof of concept, perhaps within a specific geographical area. This would have exposed the underlying issues with rule development, giving the team the space to identify the best way to overcome them while operating on a small scale. Then, armed with an understanding of what needed to be in place for rollout to be a success, rollout territories could have been defined that split the country into delivery packages engineered to minimise the negative impact on operations and the customer, allowing more attention to be paid to them while going through transition.

All too often when carrying out assurance work, I come across programmes that seem to have paid little attention to how the totality of the work should be segmented and sequenced and the lazy application of a one-size-fits-all delivery approach, leading to suboptimal performance.

Packaging

Once you have completed your strategic thinking, you should have a clearly defined business strategy, and perhaps an associated transformation strategy. You have defined your 'as is' and 'to be' business architecture, understand where gaps exist at the capability level, and have drafted a high-level, aspirational route map that illustrates some form of sequence of initiatives that you believe will deliver your wildly important business goals.

The next step is for you to take this collateral and, utilising the knowledge, skill and experience of the transformation leader, the business and technical architects and the wider team, to consider the best route to delivery. This type of thinking is what I call 'packaging'. It is common to see projects that have been long in the making become redundant as soon as they hit the market, undermined by a competitor who delivers in half the time. The product – that sales believed would be ground-breaking – and the services that surround it are often similar, but the competitor has essentially been more agile and packaged up the work in a way that has enabled them to hit the market with greater pace.

The ability to assess work, determine the most appropriate way to chunk up scope and to then associate these chunks with the most applicable delivery vehicle underpins programme delivery success. When considering how best to structure work there are many factors to consider, including:

- Reducing the scope of the work where there are negligible benefits. If something isn't considered vital now, it will inevitably get dropped when it gets tough and if it's later on in the lifecycle money will have already been spent.

- Conducting proof of concepts in a test or live environment to get early insight into what it takes to achieve success.

- Bringing forward the delivery of business benefits through the creation of a number of packages of work and delivering these into production in stages.

- Organising work so that earlier deliveries link to requirements that deliver the biggest benefit. If 80% of your benefit is delivered through the implementation of 30% of your requirements, wouldn't you want to get those to market first?

- Removing risk by identifying complex requirements and planning in early technical proof of concept activities before fully committing to a plan.

- Avoiding dependencies wherever possible, which may involve the movement of some elements of scope within the delivery schedule to a later date to give the dependency donor more time to deliver.

From how I plan my professional engagements through to how I pack my car for a holiday, the drive to organise around the achievement of a specific outcome is always present in my life. It frustrates me when I see cases, dog beds, hiking gear, shopping, camping gear and people haphazardly packed. It annoys me when I end up sitting on part of a seat which I seem to be sharing with an ice box and it finishes me off when, on arrival, I find that the things I need first are at the bottom of the pile and the lemon cake has been squashed.

The rules here are to stop and think long and hard about the best way to organise the scope of your programme to optimise delivery performance.

Right-size governance

Accepting that there are a whole range of topics that are covered under the heading of governance (including methods, tools, policies, processes, resource management, monitoring, control, quality management, risk and issue management) and that there are various sources of best practice available, I will focus on governance at the macro-level here.

In almost all my roles over the last thirty years I have been reliant upon portfolio, programme or programme management offices (PMO) for insight and control of significant investments. As my knowledge of what does and doesn't work has increased, I have become increasingly obsessed with having smaller teams focusing less on activities that I see as adding little value (for example, setting up meetings and workshops, doing administration, progress chasing and producing reports) and focusing more on stuff that really adds value.

In my ideal world the PMO function has a range of products and services that enable an organisation to deliver an optimised portfolio faster, with greater confidence and for less money. If the PMO can demonstrate the creation of value while holding others accountable for the same, then it can be considered a value-creation function able to fund its own operations and contribute to efficiencies that will enable the organisation to deliver more for less (or more for the same spend) at the portfolio level.

My version of a PMO remains small even when supporting the most complex portfolios, programmes and projects and is populated with experts who have a background in delivery and know what good looks like.

The experts set standards, define policies and practices and select and implement tools. They oversee compliance from a position of knowledge and experience rather than theory, enforcing it only where it matters. A PMO is *not* doing its job when it reviews status reports to make sure that the summary statements are precisely thirty-five words long and date formats are always of a certain format. To protect the innocent, I can't provide more context, but you know who you are.

A good friend of mine says that while the definition and application of rules is important, not parking your brain at the door is essential for an effective PMO. We may all adhere to speed limits, but if you were faced with a dangerous situation where you needed to put your foot down to get out of trouble, I am sure you wouldn't hesitate.

The right sized PMO is the home of experts with the knowledge, skills and experience to define and manage a whole range of standards and the desire to train and coach others to improve compliance and delivery performance. The type of resources that are set up and run by successful PMO operations are able to easily define and implement in alignment with the company's policies portfolio, programmes, project governance structures, policies, methods and processes. They will also be able to facilitate the ongoing management of such, providing real insight into plans, risks, issues and financial performance that underpin effective executive decision making.

They will also be able to define and own the tools and processes by which management plans are developed and maintained. They will create and own the portfolio, programme and project plan hierarchy, setting policies relating to planning standards. They will provide hands-on training and oversee compliance with policies. They will also assist portfolio, programme and project managers with the creation of the most complex scenarios, bringing to bear deep expertise in how best to formulate plans.

The PMO will be able to define and co-ordinate the stage gate process, producing the stage gate plan, review timetable and agenda. They will use their expert knowledge to conduct assessments of compliance at a deliverable level in advance of gate management events, ensuring that quality standards are adhered to. Where exceptions are agreed to allow gate transition to occur, they will follow up to ensure that agreed actions are implemented.

In conjunction with the enterprise business and technical architects, they will specify which artefacts need approval by the design authority and own the design authority plan, the review timetable and agenda. As with the stage gate process, they will use their expert knowledge to conduct assessments of compliance at the deliverable level in advance of design authority events, ensuring that quality standards are adhered to. Where exceptions are agreed, they will follow up to ensure that agreed actions are implemented. If your

PMO doesn't sound like this, then it's probably admin heavy and value light.

Less is more

A number of years ago a colleague of mine worked with a large financial institution that had invested in the setup of an Enterprise Portfolio Management Office (EPMO). The organisation had employed a sizeable team of thirteen PMO analysts, officers and managers to look after a portfolio that was fairly small in size, with an average annual investment spend of less than £50m. Despite having a big team, there was a history of projects generally failing to achieve results promised within agreed timeframes and costs. As an alternative model, a bank that I worked with had a programme supporting a similar level of spend with just two incredibly talented people in its PMO. The programme also had a track record of delivery within timeframes and costs. Why was the large EPMO team unable to deliver the right outcomes while the small PMO was able to deliver consistently? The table below provides some insight into the different characteristics of the two teams:

Characteristics of the larger EPMO	Characteristics of the smaller PMO
The team spends 10% of their working week attending meetings where there are no defined inputs or outputs.	The team spends 20% of their working week at the programme level defining and reviewing policies and practices and providing training and coaching to the wider team on best practice. (Focusing on how things are done.)
The team spends 30% of their working week in various project meetings taking minutes, noting down actions and making updates to risk, assumption, issue and decision (RAID) logs.	The team spends 30% of their working week at the programme level on the co-ordination of the main programme oversight board, the design authority and stage gate transition process.
The team spends 20% of their working week on general administration for themselves and the wider portfolio team, including room bookings, travel and accommodation. (EPMO as a personal assistant.)	The team spends 30% of their working week at the project level carrying out plan, RAID, estimation, cost and other forms of compliance reviews, making sure that what they do there is done well, identifying problems and finding solutions.
The team spends 20% of their working week on the production of various packs, including a board report with over 130 pages.	The team spends 20% of their working week on self-development attending seminars, learning from their peer network and taking on job developmental assignments.
20% is unaccounted for.	

Characteristics of the larger EPMO	Characteristics of the smaller PMO
The team is populated by:	The team is populated by:
People with an average of fifteen years of service, settled in their ways, afraid of change, somewhat out of touch with best practice and with little or no external interaction with the wider professional community.	Professional PMO resources that move between large programmes, constantly learning from the wider professional community and engaged in best practice groups.
Inward-looking with little interaction with the wider professional community and not that interested in becoming more professionally competent.	
Too many people and too many management layers with a focus on people rather than work management.	

In the example above, the EPMO is full of busy people who are glorified administrators with little or no portfolio, programme or project expertise. They are busy doing stuff with questionable value, running around saying how stressed they are while adding negligible value. As a result, the wider programme and project community see the EPMO team as an overhead, complain about their interference and laugh at their lack of understanding. The resources are not expensive when compared to project managers and other resources who they supposedly support, but let's do the maths.

There are thirteen people with an average salary of £35k, which adds up to nearly half a million pounds per annum (and that's without overheads).

As you can imagine, the smaller PMO is a different place. It runs to a tight schedule with both members of the team able to manage and prioritise their workload. The team have come from a delivery background with real-life experience and are seen by the wider professional community as adding value. The average cost per resource is £80k per annum, which can seem expensive with the PMO costing £160k, but it's less than half of the cost of the poorly performing EPMO. More importantly, it delivers value every day.

If you want to free up your programme and project manager's time through the provision of administration support, then I suggest you hire a PA. It doesn't make sense to make this part of your control function; it dilutes the professional standing of the team. A colleague sums this up nicely, saying, 'How can I really govern your work if I also fetch your tea and sandwiches?'

Data management

Another common cause of failure in the context of portfolio, programme and project offices is the failure to capture, analyse and use insight effectively.

HE SAID SHE SAID

A colleague worked with a large insurance organisation during a period where there was a significant data migration exercise underway. The migration, which was triggered as a result of a business acquisition, was considered to be the most strategically important investment being made across the portfolio of change. The executives all seemed to be aware that the programme was in difficultly, with most saying that it was well behind schedule. The business programme manager attended regular programme board meetings and reported slippages in technical deliverables, pointing a finger at the IT function. Everyone would pile in and give the IT director a hard time. Armed with his own set of slides, he would then point the finger right back at the business programme manager, citing issues with business deliverables as being to blame for delays. The board were confused about what was actually causing the delays and nobody was taking the action needed to resolve them.

All too often when programmes are in trouble, we see competing information being presented, with person A's view being out of line with person B's view and both of them being out of line with their key supplier's view. If your PMO is set up properly then this should not be possible. Great decision support is underpinned by having a clear agreement about the data to be captured, who will capture the data, when it will be captured and where (ideally, we have a single source of truth).

Performance analysis should be carried out by the PMO without bias and packs produced for governance bodies such as programme boards that contain facts, not feelings. I dislike it when people say, 'We hope...' (hope isn't a management tool), 'We assume...' (makes an ass out of you and me) and, 'We believe...' (I'm not a child talking about fairies).

You also need to be brave, as it is not easy to share failures. Where things are late, encourage the wider team to be transparent and factual as this allows everyone to gain a common understanding of the state of play and to move on at pace towards resolving prevailing issues. This approach requires programme leaders and their teams to face issues rather than obfuscating and looking for others to blame. The mantra is 'we all succeed or fail together'.

Clearly defining a set of KPIs with a balance between lead measures (indicators of future performance that allow for action to be taken in a pro-active manner if tracking outside of tolerance) and lag measures (these focus on what has gone before that and cover the scope of the management office function as well as the portfolio with its programmes and projects) is the right place to start. Although the final set of KPIs may differ between organisations, it usually contains a mix of completion rates (planned versus actual time, cost and quality), success rates (planned versus actual desired benefits and outcomes), resource utilisation, management of risk and management of conflict.

What you really need to avoid is sitting in a transformation programme board being walked through long-winded, eighty-page slide decks covering intricate details of every project. Governance boards should be focused on the achievement of strategic goals and benefits, investment cases, critical milestones and dependencies and high-level financials. They should be making the big decisions about what to start, what to stop and what to defer. If your board is hearing about the minutiae of delivery and you're spending time discussing project level performance, then governance at the next level down is not working.

Having discussed what can go wrong and what to watch out for, it is increasingly clear that a solid management office that is impartial, unbiased, with access to solid data about performance and with the ability to validate that what they are seeing represents the truth, will essentially provide you with the insight you need to avoid failure. If your management office is not providing this insight then they are probably an annoyance to all concerned.

Transformation programme management

Programmes are not large projects, nor are they portfolios of projects. They require the transformation programme director to be willing and able to make decisions in response to circumstances, with the natural ability to reshape, reconfigure and re-align solutions. A transformation programme director deals with multiple components and is able to handle conflicts that arise as a result of differing interests. They are able to influence stakeholders and be creative when it comes to problem solving. They are naturally inquisitive, asking questions and seeking insight to arrive at the right business outcome.

When it comes to transformation and/or programme directors, I increasingly find organisations making hiring decisions and onboarding people who seem to have a real lack of suitable experience. Often, they have held a role on the periphery of a programme (perhaps at an executive level) and have some understanding of concepts, but they have not got the experience and knowledge required to deliver complex transformations well. It is no wonder that we see such high degrees of failure. Where inexperienced leadership is at the helm of your transformation programme then you will see many of the causes of failure that are discussed in this book. Members of my professional community make a good living stepping in when inexperienced leaders have been employed and spent vast quantities of hard-earned cash to create nothing short of a mess. Put simply, to avoid the risk associated with lack of expertise, make sure you onboard someone with the knowledge, skills and expertise to help you deliver your transformation programme.

When looking to onboard an experienced transformation leader, in addition to the capabilities previously mentioned, look for evidence of the following:

- Ability to plan for and facilitate sessions with the executive leadership team designed to elicit a clear strategy for the organisation and build a coalition of support for the future transformation programme.

- Ability to collaborate with members of the executive team to identify proposals for investment which will deliver benefits in support of the desired strategic outcome.

- Ability to work with business architecture to define the future design of the organisation and to evaluate the size and complexity of the changes proposed based on the gap between the current and future states.

- Ability to assess the nature of individual and collective proposals and determine the best approach for packaging of work into deliverable chunks.

- Evidence of expertise in all available methods and the ability to determine and implement the programme's overarching methods and any allowable variations for each chunk of work.

- Ability to understand and work with IT architecture in the definition of the future technical design.

- Ability to engage with business architecture to define a series of transition states based on an order of delivery which depicts the evolution of the organisation and its design over the lifecycle of the transformation programme.

- Ability to mobilise the programme and its constituent projects, setting standards for governance at both programme and project levels with internal and external supplier teams.

- Ability to provide oversight and guidance to programme and project resources.

As to the hiring of transformation programme director, I urge you to seek references from previous organisations, use external networks to help identify people with a strong track record and/or ask an experienced interim to help you interview candidates and validate their qualifications and experience. Your transformation leader needs to be a practitioner. They must be attentive to details when it comes to methods, tools and processes across the broad range of disciplines. If they aren't, then who will be?

Having a deep and practical knowledge of method and practice is especially important where there are a number of suppliers being engaged. Each will have individual ways of doing things that will need to be integrated across the programme. Your leader will need to be able to weave together the internal and external supplier methods to create a cohesive, end-to-end delivery approach.

In summary, your transformation or programme director should be able to work with you and the top team to define strategic goals and then translate them into a programme vision, design a set of projects that are packaged in such a way to improve their deliverability and set out how methods (or a mix of methods) will be used. If they can't do this, they are no use to you.

If the wider team describes your programme director as 'nice', then it's a bad sign. A good leader will be strategic, knowledgeable, challenging, passionate, driven, clear-minded, political, confident, resilient, emotionally intelligent, collaborative, direct, decisive, dependency-phobic, structured and motivational. If you have worked with a person who displays these characteristics, you will know that they are rarely described as nice.

One final point on the subject of key programme leadership roles. You may have a change team in place that is able to successfully deliver your annual 'business as usual' change portfolio. The same function is unlikely to have the knowledge, skills and depth of experience required to deliver a large transformation, in particular at the top level where the skills required are different. The people that are successful leaders of truly transformational change tend to be in the consulting market, moving from organisation to organisation and bringing their independence and gravitas to critical roles. They are unlikely to accept a role as a permanent employee running an annual change portfolio, no matter how large, so the people that currently run your change function are also unlikely to be able to offer real help with the selection of the team you will need to put in place to lead your programme.

Analysis management

The International Institute of Business Analysis (IIBA) defines business analysis as 'a set of tasks and techniques used to work as a liaison among stakeholders to understand the structure, policies and operations of an organisation and to recommend solutions that enable the organisation to achieve its goals.'[10] This involves the understanding of how an organisation functions (goals, objectives, organisational unit's purpose), the capabilities an organisation requires to provide products and services to external stakeholders, the current state, and lastly, how solutions will meet business needs, goals and objectives.

Getting analysis right means that capability units are delivered where needed in the best way possible to meet a business need. Getting it wrong will lead to misalignment between the needs of the business and the scope of the programme and its component projects. When a programme gets its analysis and scope right, it's easier for this to stay front and centre of mind, acting

---

10 'The Business Analysis Profession' (IIBA UK), https://tinyurl.com /kx87f27f, accessed 21 April 2021

as true north for the team, and for the delivery risks associated with scope creep to be more easily mitigated.

A financial services organisation that I worked with would conduct a detailed and thorough review of its end-to-end customer experience in advance of any substantial investment. As part of this they would talk to users across a wider spectrum of industries and channels, resulting in improvement recommendations. Often the long list of customer experience recommendations is simply accepted, and a customer experience programme initiated to deliver them. However, in this example the executive team took a short pause to focus on the completion of work to define their business strategy. Having defined their strategy, they then moved on to review the detailed findings of the customer experience research, which were grouped into key themes. A significant subset was purposefully selected for integration with the strategy and the final set of goals for the organisation. The strategy incorporating the customer experience aligned themes and their outcomes formed the basis of a new strategic transformation programme. With this approach, when questions arose about a particular need and if this need was being satisfied by the programme, it was easy to see if it aligned with the original subset of recommendations and their outcomes. It was just as easy to stop the changes that didn't make the cut during the strategic review. Vision-based programmes with a clear strategic link, and a set of specific goals and outcomes enable good scope definition at outset.

As discussed earlier, emergent programmes (where initiatives have emerged in a piecemeal fashion as a business has been forced to respond to events as they arise) are often less strategic in nature. Emergent programmes can be among some of the most difficult to fix and require the most experienced resources as the new leader will need to find ways to create the required structures and frameworks and to integrate the various streams of work while projects are in full-on delivery mode (ie, changing the wheels while the bus is in motion). The focus for these programmes should be to transition them as quickly as possible into a vision-based programme and to get the new scope defined and baselined as part of this.

What does great scope management look like? Programmes focus on delivery of large strategic goals and are made up a range of projects that deliver improvements to capabilities. In turn, these deliver benefits that collectively match the needs defined as part of the strategy and take a wide organisational and strategic view. Programmes are substantially different to projects, which are more inwardly focused on the completion of tasks and the delivery of work products.

There is a natural tension between the strategic programme and its constituent projects, with the latter wanting to aid in delivery by strict adherence to scope boundaries and the former possibly under pressure to respond to changing circumstances driven by the evolution of the business strategy. Great scope management in the programme and project sense are thus somewhat different in nature. A well-run programme needs to work out how best to walk the line between providing constituent projects with stability and predictability, while retaining flexibility to accommodate changing needs. This approach essentially relies on having great stakeholder relationships, which are built on a common understanding of what's really important and an understanding that unless resources are boundless, you can't have 100% confidence and 100% flexibility.

At the programme level, the business architect will play a vital role in the setting and allocation of scope to projects. They work with the projects and oversee analysis efforts, ensuring that projects are delivering the required scope and that they remain aligned throughout the delivery lifecycle. If changes occur that need to be aligned to projects, they will ensure that projects carry out impact analysis and that the implications of accepting a change into scope are understood. They can also act as a gatekeeper, reviewing business analysis work product to check alignment with approved scope and removing areas of scope creep and low priority and/or low benefit changes.

Before I move on, I want to talk briefly about another common problem which underpins failure to deliver benefits. As anyone who has been involved in a project will tell you, things don't always go according to plan, in particular, when they start out trying to deliver everything that everyone wants. In this type of scenario, analysis seems endless and eventually, to make progress, key users end up having to review the list of stuff to be delivered and removing the 'nice to have' stuff. When analysis concludes and the project moves into the next stage, it again runs into difficulty and the key users are asked to prioritise again, which they try to do without losing too much of the functionality needed. Then, during the test phase, bugs arise and key users are asked to prioritise fixes on the basis that not everything can make the cut. By the end of the process the scope is smaller than at outset and as a result of the cuts, benefits set out in the business case are not realisable. I refer to this as 'death by a thousand cuts' and it's more common that you might believe.

The only way to ensure that this doesn't happen to you is to have clear traceability between benefits and requirements and then for everyone to fiercely protect them during delivery. If you are a sponsor, you are on the hook. Don't allow people to extract decisions relating to scope from you or your trusted product owner or key users without providing the facts about potential benefit impacts.

Supplier selection

Suppliers come in many shapes and sizes, delivering anything from software as a service (SaaS), bespoke technology, system integration services (SI), programme project and PMO services, testing services, building, facilities, telecommunications, people, training and similar. It is no wonder that large investment programmes often find themselves in need of specific assistance with the selection of new suppliers, implementation of their product or services and embedding of them into their 'business as usual' supplier management processes.

The deal

We have all been there at some point – struggling to get a delivery across the line with unhappy users questioning whether that shiny new system that seemed so great during the selection process can seem so unable to meet the requirements of the business during delivery, and a supplier who appeared flexible and committed during bidding failing to offer up creative solutions to real-life user problems at this later stage.

If we accept that suppliers don't set out to do a bad job and users don't set out to be awkward, then we have to examine what is really going on. What are the underlying problems and what practical steps can be taken to avoid having to deal with these issues? A good place to start is with the commercials, as they may be driving the wrong behaviours. During the request for price process, were the top three contenders asked to provide a best and final offer? Did the successful supplier end up winning the deal, but at a margin that's so thin that they need to do as little as possible to configure their product to suit your business's specific needs? If this is the case, then don't be surprised when change requests become the norm and arguments about business requirements being in or out of the contracted scope become a regular feature of your day-to-day supplier interactions.

A LOSE-LOSE DEAL

Some years ago, I was working with a supplier of a well-known automated decision engine. They had a great product which had been successfully implemented numerous times in the well-established market in the USA and we agreed that we would work together to enhance the software. This would provide us with a market-leading capability and the supplier with working software suited to the lucrative UK market. We started out by holding a series of joint workshops in advance of finalising the deal to draw out high-level requirements. Then we created a clearly defined statement of work and signed contracts on this basis, fixing the price.

Sound OK? Well, 'the devil is in the detail' springs to mind. Things that looked simple at first proved to be much more complex and despite having a great relationship with the supplier and a shared desire to crack on and deliver a fantastic product, we found ourselves in trouble. In reality, the deal sucked commercially for the supplier and our scope became the battleground.

The supplier was in a position where, after ten months, they were not able to satisfy our detailed requirements. Having spent the project budget, they were in financial difficulty and were self-funding under the fixed price arrangement. They were still a long way from being able to go live with our installation, which needed to take place before they could move ahead with their launch into the UK market. At the time the programme manager, shoulder to the wheel, continued to push for more from the supplier. The programme did eventually arrive at its destination, but it took far longer than planned. To manage costs, the supplier dug in, attempted to bounce every idea and ran the implementation with an ever-reducing number of team members as they tried to keep their internal costs under tight control. The project took six months longer than necessary to implement and went well over the original budget. To add insult to injury, twelve months of benefits were also lost.

In my experience, there is no point in doing a deal with a supplier that is not commercially sound for all parties, especially where you intend to have a long-term relationship. If you have a contract in place that is driving the wrong behaviour, then you really need to stop what you are doing and work with the supplier to re-imagine a better, more sustainable arrangement and then do your damnedest to make it happen.

Objective alignment

Check to make sure that your procurement team's objectives are not driving behaviours that will undermine your programme. If, for example, your procurement function rewards their team based on savings made, then team members have a good incentive to start out with looking for highball prices, allowing them to drive down hard through the selection process to achieve the biggest 'saving' possible. The gap between the silly highball and the flawed lowball might look like a procurement success, but we all know that when something looks too good to be true, it probably is. Make sure any deal is win/win with both the parties benefiting from the deal in the short, medium and longer-term.

Scope and suppliers

A rich source of work for transformation experts is associated with assurance and the turnaround of failing programmes, with work being initiated when organisations realise that they need help to diagnose what has gone wrong and help to address underlying causes of failure. It is common to see millions of pounds being spent on suppliers with little to show for the investment other than lots of programme, project and technical documentation. Often, many months into delivery there is no evidence of new process or working software.

One of the first things I ask to see when I evaluate a programme is some form of artefact that clearly sets out the scope of the work to be done. Responding to this request should be easily satisfied through the sharing of a high-level scope document that sets out key requirements and makes a clear link to programme or project benefits and which has ideally been signed off by the sponsor and product owner. If I can't see a scope document and I'm told that it's not relevant as the programme is 'agile', I smile. Anything large, regardless of delivery method, needs to know when there has been sufficient delivery for the product to achieve its benefits. We don't start out building a house without a plan and it wouldn't be much use if we stopped before the roof was on. Without an agreed scope it is impossible to manage delivery, particularly when we need to assess new requirements as being either in or out of scope.

When programmes are in trouble it is usual to see requirement changes being raised and decisions being made based on whether the item is thought of as important rather than being directly within scope and attaching to core benefits. My experience is that everything raised is likely to be seen as vital by someone somewhere within the wider stakeholder community. When out of control, the work stack just keeps growing, delivery timescales just keep moving, and of course costs keep spiralling out of control.

Lack of understanding of scope and control of requirements is unforgivable. I am reminded of a project which needed turning around for a large finance company. A well-known system integrator had been engaged for over twelve months at a cost in excess of £15m with no tangible output. It was immediately obvious that the scope of the project was far from clear, with business units across the globe adding their specific requirements without any control of scope. As a result, the supplier was in an endless cycle of assessing and costing what they saw as new work and producing change requests for approval and replanning. I could say that the system integrator should have known better and been more professional, but in this case, the customer was really at fault.

I also worked with another institution where the product and marketing teams were well known for saying, 'Well it makes sense to do this while the bonnet's open,' (usually an idea that on its own wouldn't pass muster) and packing the scope with all sorts of changes. While there can be benefits associated with consolidating changes that impact a particular feature of a system, there are also downsides. After all, it's additional change that uses up investment spend that may be better spent elsewhere, and whatever anyone says, it's a distraction for the team who need to stay focused if delivery is to progress effectively.

I focus on scope in this section about suppliers because it's a real cause of failure. Mismanagement of scope is bad enough when feeding internal teams with development but it's terrible when it's feeding suppliers. Suppliers have no incentive to say no, especially when a contract is on a time and materials basis, with extra work linked to increased fees. If you find yourself in this position, it isn't your supplier out of control, it's a self-management failure. Define your scope clearly and work with your supplier to avoid stepping outside of agreed scope boundaries.

Keeping control

It's common to see multiple suppliers engaged when large transformation programmes are underway and to see a real lack of clarity around roles and responsibilities between inhouse and supplier teams, leading to the mismanagement of deliverables and dependencies. This mess often becomes most apparent when programmes become stuck in the test phase, with various suppliers arguing about bugs that have been raised and whose code is responsible.

Programme and project management is responsible for ensuring that there is a clear picture of who is accountable for what, illustrated through the use of a RACI matrix or similar. Procurement assist, ensuring that suppliers are engaged in defining and agreeing their specific sections of the RACI from the outset, as well as agreeing how handoffs between teams will be handled and how common standards and policies will be applied, among other things.

Successful supplier management in the transformation arena requires knowledge and skill, which develops with experience. Where procurement has the required capabilities then it is usual for someone to be seconded into a transformation programme, perhaps on a full-time basis, supported by the wider procurement team and operating under the standard corporate processes and policies. If expertise is not readily available, then experienced contract procurement professionals are readily available. The programme level supplier manager role is vital as they co-ordinate the selection of critical suppliers, lead contract negotiations, provide oversight of the contract agreement process and set supplier standards. Having someone on the team that understands how to get the best out of your suppliers will pay dividends.

Summary checklist

To achieve a successful set up, aim for:

- Supplier deals: A well-constructed set of deals that are win/win in nature and a clear picture of who is accountable for what in terms of delivery, underpinned by robust supplier management that enables delivery of the required business outcomes.

- Cohesive packaging: Has programme leadership got the ability to assess work and determine the most appropriate way to chunk-up programme scope and to associate chunks with the most applicable delivery vehicle?

- Solid programme leadership. Has your programme leader:

- Reduced the scope of the work where there are negligible benefits?

- Carried out proof of concepts in a test or live environment to get early insight into what it takes to achieve success?

- Brought forward the delivery of business benefits through the creation of a number of packages of work delivered into production in stages?

- Organised work so that earlier deliveries link to requirements that deliver the biggest benefit?

- Removed risk by identifying complex requirements and planning in early technical proof of concept activities before fully committing to a plan, and avoided dependencies wherever possible?

• Right-size governance: Is your management office the home of real experts with the knowledge, skills and experience to define and manage a whole range of standards and the ability to train and coach others to improve compliance and delivery performance?

• Less is more: Is your management office as small as it can possibly be and running to a tight schedule with members of the team able to manage and prioritise their workload and seen as value-adding by the wider professional community?

- Data management: Is your decision support underpinned by the right data set and captured by the right people at the right time? Is there a single source of truth?

- An open work culture: Are people who report unafraid and able to be transparent and factual?

- KPIs: Are key performance indicators in place with a balance between lead and lag measures?

- Board behaviour: Are your governance boards focusing on making the big decisions (what to start, what to stop and what to defer) and the big programme level risks and issues or are they talking about project level matters?

- Transformation leadership: Do you have someone leading your transformation who has a track record of successfully running programmes rather than being on the periphery?

- Deliverability: Is your transformation or programme director able to work with you and the top team to define strategic goals? Are they able to translate this into a programme vision, design a set of projects that are packaged in such a way to improve their deliverability and set out how methods (or a mix of methods) will be used?

- Clear analysis management: Is the scope of your programme clear and is it front and centre of mind, acting as true north for the team?

- Flexibility: Has the programme worked out how best to walk the line between providing constituent projects with stability and predictability while retaining flexibility to accommodate changing needs?

- Sound architecture models: Are business and technical architecture playing a role in the governing of scope at project level, ensuring alignment with programme-level approved business and technical architecture models?

- Traceability: Is there clear traceability between the strategic goals, programme goals, project objectives and benefits, scope, and associated requirements? Are decisions around prioritisation made with full knowledge of the impact on costs and benefits?

- Appropriate suppliers: Is the deal a win/win deal with sufficient benefit for all parties involved and is it driving the right behaviours?

- Objective alignment: Are the objectives of everyone involved in the procurement process aligned and driving the right behaviours?

- Clear scope boundaries: Is the supplier scope clear and are there controls in place with suppliers to avoid them stepping outside of scope boundaries?

- Balanced expertise: Does the programme have sufficient dedicated procurement expertise to co-ordinate the selection of critical suppliers, lead contract negotiations, provide oversight of the contract agreement process and set supplier standards?

FOUR

Delivering

We have spent time setting out our strategy, evaluating and agreeing initiatives that we want to progress, defining our 'as is' and 'to be' architectures, chunking up our work into projects, defining our delivery route map and our transition states. In the chapter Setting Up For Success, we talked about packing work into deliverable chunks that are tight in terms of scope (doing the right things), that bring forward delivery of benefit and limit exposure to risks and dependencies.

In the first section of this chapter, I want to draw your attention to the need for delivery flexibility. When I hear that a programme is waterfall or agile, I worry. More often than not, in my experience complex programmes achieve optimised results by utilising a mix of different delivery methods. Taking into account the characteristics of the initiative proposed, an experienced transformation leader must be able to conduct some form of delivery mode assessment and align the work with the most suitable delivery methodology. If they are unable to do this then you have an essential skills gap which will need to be filled. Delivery method should be decided by those 'nerdy change people' you employ. If your executive team are talking methodology and debating the pros and cons of dynamic systems development methods versus Scrum, then something is wrong.

I am personally method agnostic, although I accept that current trends tend towards agile methodology.

Waterfall

Most of you will have come across waterfall, which is a tried and tested methodology generally seen as linear in approach. Stakeholder and customer requirements are gathered at the beginning of the project, with a sequential project plan being created to accommodate the full set of approved requirements. The waterfall approach was first conceived by Winston W Royce in 1970,[11] and it was adopted quickly by many industries because its logical sequencing is easy to understand and to implement.

Waterfall has somewhere between five to seven phases that follow a strict linear order, where a phase generally doesn't begin until the previous phase has been

---

11   Dr WW Royce, 'Managing the development of large software
      systems', (reprinted from *Proceedings*, IEEE, August 1970),
      https://tinyurl.com/s2ps82dc, accessed 25 May 2021

completed. The specific names of the phases generally vary from company to company and don't really matter as long as everyone engaged understands what they mean.

Waterfall is often seen as old-fashioned, with other methods being seen as delivering faster results. It is easy to see why this perception has become the norm as organisations that tend focus on this method also seem to favour fairly rigid delivery schedules with quarterly releases or similar, which are often seen as a way for technology functions to drive efficiency. Change generally joins the release schedule at a set point in time with all items exiting the release vehicle at the same time, regardless of size. One organisation I worked with had a fifteen-month delivery cycle with small changes requiring only days of effort being tied into the development cycle of major projects, meaning that they took over a year from idea to delivery. This obviously doesn't make sense.

Having a rigid and efficient cycle is not problematic for markets where change is infrequent but for dynamic businesses where competitors are innovating daily, this lack of pace is a threat to retaining or improving a competitive position.

Iterative approaches

As an alternative to waterfall, many organisations favour the use of more iterative approaches. Iterative tends to work well when the high-level scope is known and there is an opportunity to deliver some value early by breaking up the project into chunks for implementation. Often the first iteration delivers a simple implementation which then progressively gains more complexity and a broader feature set until the final system is complete.

A large financial organisation wanted to implement Salesforce across its numerous business units. Taking an iterative approach enabled them to deliver quickly to a number of business units that serviced simple products, with subsequent iterations offering increased functionality enabling rollout to the more complex business units. This approach provided value early in the lifecycle. It also gave early adopters of the new system the opportunity to provide the programme team with improvement suggestions, with great ideas being incorporated into each successive iteration delivered. In a waterfall world nobody would have received working software until everything defined was available and the opportunities to realise early benefits and learn early lessons based on user feedback would have been lost, which is why this approach is so attractive.

Agility

I am sure that most people at this point will expect me to say something about agile methodology, but I find myself struggling to say anything that is fundamentally different to my thoughts on iterative. Technologists have been developing agile ways of working for over thirty years, so it is more an evolution than a revolution. There are lots of consulting firms and people in the marketplace selling agile frameworks to organisations when at times the organisation isn't ready or the portfolio of work isn't really suited.

I have worked with organisations that have spent vast sums attempting to implement agile with little success. Often the methods are more suited to software development houses rather than organisations that specialise in selling consumer finance, insurance or health care. If you don't have the capability, you won't be able to develop it fast, so you may need to think about partnering with a company that specialises in software delivery to provide the capability as a service.

Rather than implementing a one-size-fits-all method, your goal should be to meet the needs of your programme and its constituent projects using tools and techniques taken from the agile school along with waterfall and other disciplines, underpinned by the right behaviours. As the speed of change increases, most businesses need to improve agility, but not all businesses need agile.

I want to briefly return to underpinning ways of working that need to be in place for a transformation programme to succeed.

When I help organisations with agile implementation, I hear a lot about method, frameworks, processes and tools. I hear much less about principles. Even a transformation programme that employs a mix of waterfall, iterative and agile methods can be benefit from the underlying principles of agile, which focus on continuous delivery, direct communication, self-organisation, trust, technical and design excellence and simplicity, among others.[12] (The full 'Principles behind the Agile Manifesto' can be found at https://agilemanifesto.org/principles.html).

I am of the firm belief that embedding as many of these principles as possible within any organisation will improve change performance, regardless of delivery method.

People from various disciplines quote selectively from the Agile Manifesto to suit their purpose; I have heard many people in senior roles argue, 'We are running project X as an agile development, so we aren't bothering with process, documentation and planning.' This shows a lack of understanding of the Manifesto which, while it values 'individuals and interactions', 'working software' and 'responding to change' more highly, does acknowledge the value of processes and tools, documentation and planning too.[13]

---

12   M Beedle et al, 'Principles Behind The Agile Manifesto',
      https://agilemanifesto.org/principles.html, accessed 21 April 2021
13   M Beedle et al, 'Manifesto For Agile Software Development',
      https://agilemanifesto.org, accessed 21 April 2021

Delivery mode assessment

Moving away from method (more specifically, agile) to that all-important delivery mode assessment that we touched on earlier. When carrying out an assessment it is useful to consider the characteristics of each initiative, as the characteristic will generally help to determine the most appropriate delivery method:

Towards Iterative	Towards Waterfall
The customer is hands-on and able to be part of the team throughout the project.	The customer provides input at key stages (eg, reviews requirements, business rules) and gets engaged in user acceptance testing.
Change is welcomed, accepting that this comes with cost.	
Scope is not fully known or fixed.	Scope is known in advance and fixed.
Features can be prioritised and there is an acceptance that not everything has to be delivered by a certain date.	Everything in scope has to be delivered.
Customer feedback is obtained early and often and is seen as essential to delivering the right commercial end state.	Team co-ordination is limited to handoff points (large/ complex set of on and offshore teams)
Smaller, dedicated multi-skilled teams with a high degree of collaboration.	Reducing risk to a firm, fixed contract is important.
Contact, both internal and external, is on a time and materials basis.	Funding is linked to features which are linked to benefits.
Funding is not linked to features.	

Most projects fall somewhere on the continuum between iterative and waterfall characteristics and so they may benefit from a tailored approach to delivery by phase. As an example, I was involved some time ago in the delivery of a new data capability for a large financial organisation. The project was mobilised working with a third-part software vendor as a waterfall initiative with the core implementation of product components and interfaces being fully delivered in a linear (waterfall) manner. Alongside this, a series of sprints were defined to deliver iteratively once the core capability was in place with the data and reporting requirements giving early access to valuable operational data and insight. The final stage of method evolution saw the project transition to full agile for ongoing business improvements.

A key message I want you to take away from this section of the book is that one size doesn't fit all when it comes to delivery method. This is inefficient and ineffective and limits your flexibility. In addition, it's important not to be swayed by what's in fashion. I also want to stress that when I talk about choice of method, flexibility and tailoring of method at the project level, I am not talking about creating a Frankenstein's monster that strings together bits of different methods in a way that nobody understands.

If your transformation leader is unable to assess and set up your programme of work using the right mix of methods to deliver the results you need then you will need to consider options to address this gap. It is worth noting that the skills needed to initiate a programme are different from those needed to turn the handle once the programme's constituent projects are all in flight, so the best option with the biggest payback is to consider onboarding a partner (perhaps án interim) to help you safely navigate this phase.

Method integration

Where we have complex transformation programmes, we frequently have a range of internal and external suppliers that will have their own ways of doing things, including the processes and tools used. Suppliers will usually have a degree of flexibility allowing them to tailor their approach, although too much variation is not desirable as it may have a negative impact on delivery as they learn to work with processes that they are less familiar with. In terms of tools, it is common to see a mix of industry standard tools, for example, Jira (www.atlassian.com/software/jira; part of a family of products designed to help teams manage work) or Confluence (www.atlassian.com/software/confluence; useful as a project collaboration tool).

What is important is for tooling strategies to be as clear as possible with a high degree of alignment between teams enabling them to work together, ideally with a single source of truth, to deliver a unified end solution. Programme leadership should be able to select the best toolset taking into account the nature of the work as well as the approaches favoured by key suppliers, and to work with suppliers to make sure that they understand what is required.

DON'T NEEDLESSLY COMPLICATE IT

An organisation that I spent some time working with had stable change and IT functions, both of which had developed over time and were well embedded yet had separate lifecycles. The key stages within the lifecycles were different and the deliverables required to transition gates were out of line.

The two processes were essentially operating independently, with their own set of rules and management information relating to the deliverables required by each stage and stage entry and exit criteria. As a result of the lifecycle misalignment, reporting of progress between change and IT was at times contradictory and application of more mature governance was impossible. The problem was fairly easy to address through process redesign in collaboration with the change and IT teams.

It may seem like focusing on method and process at outset is slowing down progress when everyone is keen to just get going, but starting out without having a clear and shared understanding will eventually hit productivity.

Productivity and planning

We have all seen programmes that appear highly productive (picture lots of stressed-out people, endless meetings and workshops, regular show and tell sessions, more reports than you can possibly digest and enough documents to fill the British library), but are in fact hiding the bitter truth that they are slow, unproductive and failing.

As executives we are used to seeing operational productivity and service level data and it would be hard to imagine a world where we have no idea of the state of, for example, the sales pipeline, the number of calls, emails or online hits per minute/hour/day and the achievement of associated response service levels.

Programmes are made up of projects. Projects have deliverables that are captured in plans and associated with start and end dates, so it is easy to check at both the project and rolled-up programme level if deliverables planned within a specific period have been achieved. When assessing the health of a programme of work I look for a programme plan that contains a set of programme level deliverables alongside project key deliverables/milestones. These must be dynamically linked to underlying plans, with updates made by project leaders on a regular basis and instantly available. I expect all deliverables to be associated with resources and effort estimates and for progress towards completion to be updated at least weekly.

At the next level and while discussing plans with key parties, I look for evidence that deliverable producers have been consulted and involved in agreeing effort and timescales when plans are formulated.

Despite there being a number of well-known and affordable tools on the market and training available in the production of product-based plans and associated disciplines, almost without exception I see programme and project professionals producing sketchy plans that read like task lists, often in Excel or PowerPoint. Sponsors and executive oversight boards are often responsible for bad practice. As a sponsor, it's important to understand that the 'plan on a page' slides produced for your project board have zero value to the actual programme team and that the time they spend manipulating 1,000 milestone diamonds and lines in PowerPoint is time they are not spending managing their actual plans. As a sponsor, ask for access to the main programme plan, ideally via one of the online tools that are readily available. For example, with membership, Smartsheet (www.smartsheet.com) allows multiple plans to be created and linked and hundreds of collaborators to be given various types of access via laptop and mobile devices. Products like Smartsheet require minimal training, which means sponsors can dive in and access plans to see how they are being managed and maintained.

If programme leadership is unable to provide you with access to well developed, deliverable-based plans at programme and project level that are automatically linked to make maintenance easy and underpinned by effort estimates, then you have a problem. Without deliverable-based plans it will be impossible to work out how much has been achieved and if productivity is on track. If your programme doesn't have a proper plan then stop and onboard an experienced planning resource.

Monitoring

In the context of programme management, productivity is about the completion of planned deliverables at both programme and project level in alignment with estimated effort and within planned timescales.

There are a lot of things inaccurately termed as productivity. For example, the type of work carried out by accounting to summarise time recorded by programme resources to carry an internal cost apportionment between IT and other parts of the business. Time recording and a comparison between planned versus actual time spent on a deliverable is important. It gives us insight into the accuracy of our estimation processes and allows us to improve our future estimates, but this type of information does not measure programme productivity.

There are many formulas that we can use to calculate productivity based on deliverables, although they are not a substitute for having good quality deliverable-based plans with underpinning management information. I have seen complicated methods used to calculate productivity, for example, the approach set out below looks at the number of deliverables planned and the percentage complete within a period versus those actually delivered:

Planned	Actual
8 deliverables complete	6 deliverables complete
27 deliverables inflight with average completion rate of 61%	27 deliverables inflight with average completion rate of 51%

We can see that the programme in this example is underperforming, with a productivity rate of 75% for completed deliverables and 84% for inflight. If the lower than planned productivity was to continue, then plans would need to be reviewed and estimates adjusted.

Whatever the process implemented, it must underpin the regular monitoring of productivity and it should be evident at regular points where the programme and its constituent projects transition through their various stage gates. Plans in PowerPoint can't be used to manage productivity. Proper tools are needed and the team must have the skills to use them effectively.

Risk and issue management

When I am in assurance mode assessing programmes for underlying causes of failure, I frequently find that the methods being used to identify and manage risks and issues are immature and that the culture both within and beyond the programme team is driving the wrong behaviour. I have worked in many financial services organisations where there are robust and mature operational risk management practices embedded, but where programme and project risk management methodologies are far less mature. I have also worked with programme and project sponsors that don't make time to discuss and take ownership of escalated risks and issues and programme and project managers that handle risks and issues badly, seeing these as a negative reflection on the quality of their work.

Risk and issue management can be easily overlooked, so programme and project sponsors need to focus their teams on the identification and management of the risk landscape throughout the lifecycle of the project. A risk may be known in advance of initiation, it may arise at a point in time, it may persist throughout the lifecycle and it may have a material impact on delivery success if it materialises. Issues are problems to be resolved and may materially impact delivery if ignored. Risks that are ignored or have low quality mitigation action plans are more likely to transition from a risk to an issue that needs a solution. I would much rather spend time putting good quality risk mitigation in place than on issue resolution. Time spent making sure a risk is managed and making sure it doesn't materialise is an investment in future productivity.

From an issue point of view, I advise programme teams to look for early closure. Reviewing a long list of old issues is going to waste everyone's time. If the programme approach is working, then issues will have a clear action plan with owners and dates for completion. If the programme team are spending hours reviewing issues, then the process probably needs looking at. Issues should be transitory and on the issue log for as short a time as possible. Action should be taken at pace by the right people, and once resolved, be closed out promptly. In some cases, issues can hang around because the programme team are unable to resolve them. Where this is the case, they must escalate to the programme management group or their sponsor or programme board (whichever makes more sense) and agree a plan of action that can move the resolution forward at pace.

Programmes often hold risk and issue information in project level logs, which makes it difficult for the programme level team to understand the big picture without lots of manual effort to merge and analyse data. When I initiate programmes, I like to set up a shared log that underpins the programme level analysis of risk and issue status that the wider programme team can access. There are some great tools available where a programme level risk and issue log for use by the wider team and its stakeholders can easily be set up. As a sponsor it is vital that the programme team provide you with both big picture insight into total risks and issues by age, as well as detailed information about significant risks and issues and the status of their mitigation and management plans.

Summary checklist

To achieve successful delivery, aim for:

- The right mix of delivery method: A programme that is optimised to deliver effectively and that uses a mix of delivery methods that all parties within the delivery matrix are ready, willing and able to operate.

- Competent delivery mode assessment: Do you have an experienced transformation leadership able to conduct a delivery mode assessment that takes the characteristics of the proposed changes into account, so the work is aligned with the most suitable delivery methodologies?

- Delivery expertise: Whatever the methods selected, do you have the knowledge and skills to make them a success? If you don't have the capability, have you considered partnering with a company that specialises in software delivery to provide the capability as a service?

- Maturity: Are you aware of your change maturity level and do you understand what this means in terms of ability to deliver a complex programme of change?

- Agile principles: Are as many of the agile principles as possible being embedded within the organisation to improve change performance regardless of delivery method?

- Control of delivery methods: If your programme has projects that fall somewhere on the continuum between iterative and waterfall and which benefit from a tailored approach to delivery by phase, are you sure that the variations will still deliver?

- Delivery method integration: Are all suppliers (both internal and external) integrated in terms of method? Are they sharing the same methods, processes and tools wherever possible?

- Reliable productivity measures: Are deliverable-based, integrated plans in place that make it possible to measure productivity? Is productivity checked at least at the point of transition between stage gates (or more frequently) and are plans updated to reflect any variation?

- Clear and available plans: Are plans easily available and understandable to project, programme and stakeholder communities?

- Transparent risk management: Are risk and issue logs up to date and readily accessible by the programme team and stakeholders? Are risks and issues being closed out in a timely manner?

- Escalation procedures. Are critical risks and issues being escalated to appropriate governance bodies for action?

FIVE

Embedding

Transformational change is often driven by the need to address opportunities aligned to strategic objectives. Transformation programmes are initiated and made up of projects that deliver change. We have discussed how to define the strategic foundation that underpins change, how to create and shape a deliverable programme of work, and which methods are best suited to the nature of the work. When implemented, change delivers benefits. We have touched on the importance of these benefits, in particular, how benefit erosion throughout the lifecycle should be avoided. Now we need to discuss the part that change management, training, coaching and successful service introduction play in securing benefit realisation.

Change management

Projects within the programme will be ready to implement changes into the organisation at a number of points. This is where a lack of real change management capability can result in poor preparation in advance of change implementation as well as low impact post-implementation support. This can lead to resistance, which inevitably causes delays, undermining the delivery of business case benefits.

Change management is a discipline in its own right and comes with its own set of capabilities, methods, tools and deliverables. It is focused on changes that impact people, in particular, things that affect ways of working. It puts people, culture and behaviours front and centre. It aligns with other disciplines, including training and communications, to create a holistic colleague experience. Not all projects within a programme require the same degree of change management, but it is important to understand that changing technology is simple – it's changing of behaviours that is difficult.

As an example, a programme that was linked to improving profitability for a large insurance company had initiated a project that increased the number of decimal points used in the production of automatically produced actuarial calculations. The project required a whole raft of somewhat technical system changes, but it had no material impact on the day-to-day lives of the business community. Within the same programme, there was a project elsewhere that focused on improving the productivity of policy administration. The project was responsible for the implementation of new processes and technology that impacted over 500 staff. The need for change management in the first example was low, involving some simple communication activities, but in the second example the need was high. The second project impacted a large community and the improvements in productivity were realised through a 20% reduction in service roles. Managing this type of scenario (where the implementation of change is associated not just with the need for people to embrace new ways of working, but to do this while those impacted are facing an uncertain future with potential job losses) is difficult to manage and requires exceptional change management skills.

A word or two here about the psychology of change and how our minds work. The brain is made up of about 86 billion neurones which store and transmit information constantly (estimated connections are in excess of 100 trillion). Every time we learn new information or perform a new activity these neurones change, making new connections. As we repeat things, patterns of activity start to create pathways in the brain which enable the mind to act without conscious control over time (a bit like riding a bike; once you have learned to do it, you never forget). When we change things, we have to create new pathways and the brain uses more energy when it's having to direct operations instead of running on autopilot. The effort associated with this can be stressful, especially when we are trying to break away from well-worn pathways and taking new information and practices on board. Change is difficult and can't be ignored.

The change manager

Change management is not done by the project manager off the side of their desk, it is present in its own right throughout the lifecycle of any project. Where requirements are being defined in the early stages, change management will focus on the preparation for change (including the design of the change management strategy and the setting up of the change management team). The change manager will also work with the project sponsor to identify change champions in positions of influence within functions impacted to provide them with the training required to enable them to coach their colleagues. It is really important to understand that people impacted by change want to hear about it from their direct managers, who they know best and generally trust. Members of the impacted line management team need to be able to clearly explain and advocate for the planned changes with their teams and be taught the skills to help them deal with any resistance before, during and post-implementation.

During the lifecycle, the change manager will work with the sponsor and change champions to develop change management plans aligned to the change management strategy. These will set out the deliverables required before, during and after implementation. They will work with change champions to carry out impact assessments that help unpack the implications of the proposed changes on functions and teams, to identify potential causes of resistance to change and to agree on associated resistance management strategies.

During this phase the change manager will also work with training to weave change management strategies with training materials and strategies to create a linked and aligned approach. This will create a joined-up experience for impacted people. Finally, during implementation and training, change management will be actively collecting and analysing feedback from change champions and impacted teams. They will identify gaps and address causes of resistance. During the final stages they will actively support the sponsor and change champions in activities to reinforce the benefits change and to celebrate the success of the wider team.

Sponsors are central to change management and play a key role as the figurehead for the change. Change management will work with the sponsor to define a plan, setting out specific activities to be carried out at each stage of the project. As part of this, they will front communication with impacted staff and business leaders with the aim of building a coalition of support.

Change management is a discipline in its own right and central to the successful delivery of project and programme benefits, so why does it all too often report via the project manager? The change manager is a peer of the project manager. They have a different, yet complimentary, skillset and they should each have a direct relationship with the sponsor. Let's face facts: the project manager will not be worrying about change management deliverables in the latter stages of delivery when they are working extra hours just to get the technical delivery over the line.

Another common issue that occurs (I think in part due to a lack of understanding of the role, capabilities and deliverables of change management) is inexperienced business people being seconded into roles. Just because someone is a really great supervisor or manager, it doesn't follow that they will be able to fill the change manager gap. Unless they have gained experience in a change management role of a similar size elsewhere, they are unlikely to have the knowledge and skills required to lead as the expert in doing what's required to embed change and deliver benefits. Most organisations have a gap in terms of their change management capabilities. If you have a desire to build a change management capability and you have some time, then providing some funding for training and opportunities for trainees to work alongside tried and tested professionals will help.

Communications

In the context of change management, the worst failures occur when sponsors have the attitude that change is mandatory, and that people can either get on board or leave. Realisation of benefits may be linked to reductions in headcount, but surely keeping the people that have the highest performance and are best suited to the organisation and its future aims is preferable?

When I evaluate programme performance, I pay particular attention to poor communications as this is one of the most commonly cited reasons for programme failure. The change manager will produce plans at each stage of the change that will involve the communication of information to people. Where communications play a vital role is in matching the media to the message, creating a professional look, feel and tone and ensuring alignment of messages across the programme. They will also ensure that key messages are integrated into and not lost in the forest of more general business communications.

Common problems associated with communications range from the distance between team members as technology and working practices enable us to work from wherever we want to, handling of cultural differences between the informal tribes which exist within every organisation and that have their own behavioural norms, poor quality communication and lack of time to listen to and absorb information. For most of these problems, there are easy ways to organise communications:

Distance between team members: Members in different locations can hold live video sessions, ideally with professional facilitators for larger groups. There are a whole range of great tools available that accommodate video conferencing (eg, Zoom, WebEx, Microsoft Teams) and for larger virtual and hybrid events there are platforms like Attendify (www.attendify.com), Whova (www.whova.com) and EventMobi (www.eventmobi.com). The key with this type of communication is to work out how to get the message out there and how to get people to interact in some meaningful way as this improves the chance of communication messages sticking.

Informal tribes: When it comes to tribes, you can carry out an impact assessment to understand what aspects of change most interest or threaten specific groups and use this to inform your communications. If you want to break down barriers, you can challenge cross-tribe groups to work together to achieve a goal that will deliver value while exposing people to different streams of thought. One person's opportunity is another person's threat, so it's good to explore different perspectives.

Poor quality communication: This is common with materials that are poorly written, with incorrect grammar or complicated overall messages that are not suited to emails or posters. The fix for this is simple. Materials need to be checked to make sure that the message being communicated is suited to this type of approach, and if so, to validate its accuracy, alignment with any style guidelines and, of course, spelling and grammar.

Lack of time: I have worked in a number of organisations where communication was excellent. In each case, people were encouraged to attend briefings without feeling guilty for taking time out, given time after briefings to ask questions and motivated to talk to their teammates and leaders without fear. At the start of this chapter, I mentioned that the brain's creation of new pathways for change takes energy and time. There is no point in spending £50m on that shiny new system if people are not given time to prepare themselves for the change.

For the financially minded among us that still need to be convinced of the importance of change management, let me use this example.

THE CASE FOR CHANGE

Organisation A planned to launch a new product which would coincide with a change in regulation that opened up a new segment of the investment market. They were among a number of similar organisations wanting to get to market first to give them a better opportunity to grab market share. The project was focused on fast delivery and implemented the new system and process on time, but totally failed to prepare the organisation for the implementation properly.

People required to deal with increases in application volume were unprepared, capacity was unavailable and training had totally missed the mark, leaving people confused about what was required. This had a direct impact on productivity.

Volumes materialised as planned, which on the one hand was a cause for celebration, but behind the scenes a large backlog of customer applications was building. As the product required a fast turnaround, delays in processing resulted in applicants starting to register complaints, which drove up the volume of work further.

The post-mortem three months after implementation showed that they were unable to handle half of the volume presented. The value of the lost business was in excess of £6m. If only the sponsor had seen change management as being important. If a contract change manager had been engaged, even at top rates the cost would have been inconsequential compared to the lost revenue.

If you take nothing else away from this section, please take away that change management underpins benefit realisation. Doing it well is a skilled job and to ignore it is a false economy. Great change management combined with effective communications underpins successful transformation management. If you are interested in understanding more about change management then there are lots of resources available. A good place to start is the Change Management Institute (www.change-management-institute.com) but there are also some great consultancy organisations that excel in the provision of skilled resources in this domain.

Training

When I talk about training, I am referring to the work we do to enable others to acquire the necessary knowledge and skills to improve their ability to respond to changes to ways of working. Training may be about how we interact with processes and systems or it may be about softer things like how we behave and ways of working. The aim is to internalise the content in such a way that we become proficient in its use.

Common issues with training are:

- Lack of time to attend sessions and to absorb information post-sessions
- Distributed working and home working and the need to accommodate differing learning preferences
- A general lack of engagement if change has not been managed well
- A lack of interest in material that has little individual relevance
- A lack of budget to get the job done well.

Learning preferences

Your organisation probably has a mix of generation Z, Millennials, generation X and baby boomers, all of whom have radically different relationships with technology. When it comes to developing your training strategy, a one-size-fits-all approach that assumes that everyone is at the same tech-savvy level and has the same learning habits is unlikely to be effective. Conducting a thorough needs analysis that focuses on learning preferences and not just the knowledge required will inform training design. There are many low-cost software solutions that can be used alongside videos, written notes and graphics to cater to different learning preferences. All of these can be made available through your existing learning management system solution.

Lack of engagement

Let's assume that change management has prepared the ground and that users of the various training content and attending interventions are looking forward to getting involved and are not resistant to change. The challenge for training is then to make sure that the content being shared is relevant and seen as being important to the users. To keep energy and engagement levels up it is really important to mix learning so that there is a balance between instruction, case studies, role-plays and problem solving. It is also really important that users understand what they are expected to be able to do as a result of the intervention and that they have access to their peer group and trainers post-session to reinforce key training points.

Transformation programmes are more successful when the changes they are delivering are implemented into organisations that have an active learning culture where everyone feels involved. If your organisation doesn't have a mature learning and development capability, then the programme will need to start work on delivery of the required capabilities as early as possible.

Training that isn't relevant

This is a common problem. Training is often generic and focuses on the process, or the system or both without being personalised for specific roles. This means that users will spend time worrying about things that don't impact them while having insufficient detail about what they need to do differently. Again, the solution starts with the training needs analysis, which should be able to identify impacted roles and what core learning is needed for each part of the community.

Lack of budget

Sponsors want so much from the teams, but training budgets always seem to be squeezed. Budgets are usually made up of training personnel who carry out needs analysis work and develop content for courses and other uses, software to support online learning, and travel (including accommodation costs). Costs can be minimised through a shift to online training (which removes travel, venue and facilitation costs) as well as through adapting a content development approach that produces materials once and resumes them in different training scenarios. When a programme budget is upwards of £50m and its training workstream isn't properly funded, then someone has got their priorities wrong somewhere.

Coaching

You have carried out your training needs analysis, identified your communities and delivered interventions and content that aligns with differing learning preferences and you now have teams in the live working environment that are using the new processes and systems. What do you now need to do to support the teams? The answer is to provide coaching.

Coaching looks to improve performance in the here and now, with the coach helping individuals to improve their own performance. It is about helping people to learn rather than teaching. Coaches require a set of skills that help them to build rapport with individuals and the ability to think about problems with empathy. Coaches generally have great listening skills, are able to reflect and clarify when it comes to understanding an issue and are seen as a trusted advisor and guide by the person being coached. At times, a coach has to be brave enough to say the most difficult things about an individual's approach to a situation to help them navigate a way through to enhanced performance.

In the context of a transformation programme, it will be particularly important to decide who will provide the hands-on support once training has finished its work at project level. The ability to do this well will have a direct bearing on how quickly change will be absorbed and responded to in a positive way, and therefore a direct bearing on when benefits can start to be realised.

Service introduction

You have developed the strategy, shaped the strategic change agenda, packaged the work to improve deliverability, delivered safely, prepared the ground for the people side of change, completed user training and made the go live decision when shock... Horror... You have problems in production and the IT service desk doesn't seem able to help. What has gone wrong?

Has the programme or project focused on meeting the needs of the business users and forgotten that there is a need to also meet the needs of the teams that will support the new solution? How can this happen if the IT development team were fully engaged? A common cause of failure is driven by the way that organisations tend to segregate duties between teams that focus on project delivery and those that focus on supporting of the wider estate. Although these teams often align through the same reporting line at the top level, it doesn't follow that there will be transference of information via some sort of osmosis. Action has to be taken to ensure that service support teams are engaged in the lifecycle for new initiatives.

I like to identify the eventual service owner at the outset. This must be someone that is empowered to make decisions on behalf of the eventual support functions, able to consider service levels required and estimate how much the new service will cost to run. The same person should work with the project team to agree acceptance criteria and to ensure that service introduction deliverables are part of the project plan. In later stages of the programme or project, they should be able to assess impact on the technical functions, lead efforts to design and implement new support processes, metrics and tools, agree what needs to be documented and approved, align the service level agreement with the operational level agreements, configure tools and plan continuity arrangements. The list goes on.

Service support capability and capacity are often a problem. If your service support function is working overtime to handle 'business as usual' activities and is dependent on outdated processes and technology, then they are unlikely to be able to find the time to implement the types of changes arising from a complex transformation programme. The people that will end up servicing the technology must be engaged in every step of the programme. What can you do to free up capacity? I understand that attending a programme meeting (however critical) or producing a deliverable may be less of a priority than dealing with a production incident, so if the issue is one of capacity, then it should be fairly easy to bring in an experienced interim resource to run 'business as usual' services, allowing the right permanent resources to get involved.

The takeaway from this is that there are a whole range of things that need to be designed and implemented for IT solutions being introduced into your IT estate, and that resources need to be available and to engage throughout the programme or project lifecycle. The pace of change is increasing, and technology is evolving so the use of procedures that enable you to manage onboarding of new stuff is increasingly important. It is not something that can be thought of after the event; it needs to be properly defined, planned and implemented like any other set of change deliverables.

Capability development

All too often, programmes in the digital space look to implement technologies that are suited to iterative or agile ways of working and provide a technical foundation that enables greater business agility, but then fail to create the capabilities required to continue the process of implementing change in a 'business as usual' setting. This can be easily avoided. If you want an inhouse capability, my preferred approach is to:

1. Include an investment in your plans and costs that allows for an inhouse agility increment for each initiative. If we take Salesforce as an example, where a supplier is often selected to help with the initial heavy lifting, you could agree with them that a couple of inhouse resources be embedded into their team from the outset. They will then have a full understanding of the work that has been done and be able to carry on with development activities post-programme or project closedown.

2. Create a backlog of items during the project lifecycle that are ready to go once the project has closedown. Retain the product owner who will maintain continuity of the product and continue to drive the prioritisation of work with a full understanding of how changes will fit with the existing business solution.

Having shaped up your strategy, defined a programme, packed up work into deliverable chunks, delivered, managed change and made sure that you have the right support in place during and post-transition, you have reached the end of your delivery lifecycle. This is where all eyes shift towards the realisation of benefits and the achievement of goals.

Benefit realisation

Large changes may be driven by a need to remain compliant with regulations or to maintain technical solutions or they may be in response to a strategic ambition, for example, to improve profitability. Programmes and projects are initiated to deliver the changes and are associated with benefits, which ideally flow through following implementation.

Programmes are great at delivering stuff, but the question is, have they delivered the right stuff? Can the change actually deliver the benefits promised or are the team congratulating themselves for simply being busy and getting something done? After the hard-to-win investment budget has been secured, I see little good practice evidenced when it comes to benefit management throughout the programme or project lifecycle. There are many reasons why programmes fail to deliver promised benefits, three of which are explored here:

1. Unrealistic aspirations

2. Gone missing

3. Poor implementation

Unrealistic aspirations

The first common reason is that the benefits were unrealistic at outset. They were simply never going to happen.

This happens when sponsors are put under pressure to produce business cases with unrealistic returns on investment, resulting in unrealistic benefit assumptions.

WHERE'S THE PAYBACK?

A financial institution built a business case for a new insurance product on the basis that it would deliver a substantial number of new deals per annum, paying for itself within a twelve-month period. The project was well run and delivered to market within expected timeframes and on budget. 'Excellent,' I hear you say, but two years after launch the product was performing substantially below expectation.

Why did it go so wrong? The reality was that the product was new to the UK market and so data relating to consumer buying behaviour wasn't readily available to underpin benefit estimates. A small trial that would have provided insight into buying behaviour was proposed but written off by the sponsor as being too expensive and risky (ie, giving competitors early sight of a product that was believed to be market leading).

If the investment decision had been made at the portfolio level on the understanding that the project would focus on delivering to market first and fast and that benefit confidence levels were low as a result, that would have been OK. The board would have been presented with the facts and taken a risk. However, in this case, benefits were not called out as low confidence and the programme was allocated investment spend that could have been better used to support less risky, revenue-generating ideas.

Another issue that I see regularly is where automation delivers reductions in manual effort. This reduction is rolled up across the wider workforce and presented as a cost saving when there is no real intention, nor ability, to reduce headcount. For example, a team of 100 full-time employees follows a uniform process delivering 50 widgets per day, per person with a daily production goal of 5,000 widgets. Part of the process is automated, resulting in a 10% productivity improvement (change management challenges aside) so each person is now able to produce 55 widgets. This means that only 90.9 people are needed to deliver the same production goal. In this case, it makes sense to claim savings associated with a reduction in headcount, as long as we include the costs of redundancy in the business case, and we don't try to claim 0.1 of a person (we can't exit a finger or a hand).

You might laugh at the last bit of the example, but I see it happen regularly. As another example, let's assume we have fifteen business locations, each of which has a reception with two members of staff covering office hours. A change is implemented to move phone calls from the local branch to a central call centre. The central call centre needs an extra four heads to accommodate the increased call volume and so the business case claims a saving of twenty-six heads, making the case look attractive. If reception was just about phone calls, then that would be fine, but in practice they are about so much more (including meeting and logging in visitors, basic security admin, meeting room management), so staffing levels can't be reduced to realise these benefits.

Gone missing

The second common reason is that 'they were lost during delivery'. When programmes hit difficulties, sponsors are asked to make countless decisions about what is and isn't essential. Each decision on its own can seem immaterial, but 'death by a thousand cuts' springs to mind as the multitude of tiny compromises rolls up into a huge, benefit-crippling change. This is why the link between requirements and benefits is so important and why traceability between requirements and benefits is vital. If your programme has a handle on traceability, then as a sponsor you should be able to get hold of a proper impact analysis that considers the benefit impacts for each decision that you are being asked to make.

In the 1990s, I was nominated as the sponsor on an operation for a large system implementation just as it went live. When we went live, we had over 100 bugs, most of which affected the deliverable benefits of the system. What was worse, by the point that the non-performing beast was delivered, the business had sunk so much cash into it that there was literally nothing left to fix the mess.

In contrast, a sponsor who I worked with some years ago who was known for delivering real change set out on a mission to reduce processing costs. His team gathered requirements that could deliver the saving and produced a chart he called his 'penny benefits picture'. It clearly set out the requirements and their individual benefits. Everyone was aware of the diagram and understood the essential requirements. They knew that the sponsor was focused on benefits and this drove behaviour throughout the lifecycle.

Poor implementation

The third reason is all about failing to meet the change management challenge and ending up with a resistant workforce that are unwilling or unable to accommodate the change and/or a help desk that can't support the new software. It is never too early to start thinking about implementation and designing your approach. If you have a change that has a big impact on the way people work and their behaviours, then investing in some professional change management resources will pay dividends.

Summary checklist

When it comes to embedding change and transformation, aim for:

- The right change manager for the job: Have you got the right change management resources available? Are they engaged to design the approach to handling the human side of change at the outset of your transformation?

- A supportive sponsor: Does your sponsor have the time to work with the change management discipline to identify change champions and then to work with them and the wider community being impacted by the change?

- Appropriate training: Does your programme have a training strategy that compliments the change management strategy and does it create a set of joined-up experiences for impacted people?

- Monitoring management: Is feedback being collected pre- and post-implementation and is the information being analysed and gaps addressed and resolved?

- Clear communication: Are plans produced at each stage of the change that deliver professional content using the right media for the message and are they integrated with general corporate communications?

- Time to absorb: Are people impacted by the change able to participate fully in communications activities and are they given time to process the change messages?

- Comprehensive impact assessments: Are change impact assessments that help to unpack the implications of change on specific tribes being carried out and are 'what's in it for me' messages clearly understood?

- Quality control: Are communications of good quality? Nothing shouts 'you don't matter' more than a badly designed poster full of spelling mistakes.

- Meaningful training: Do people have sufficient time to attend training interventions and to absorb learning post-session? Does the training accommodate different learning styles, and does it cater for different working arrangements (distance versus office based)?

- Actioned feedback: Is feedback gathered on a regular basis from training interventions and analysed for gaps and issues? Are actions taken to resolve them?

- Keeping it relevant: Are training interventions tailored to suit individual needs (modular pick and mix) rather than being generic (one-size-fits-all)?

- Targeted coaching: Are people identified and trained in advance of 'go live' to offer coaching to the impacted teams? Are the coaches able to build rapport fast and seen as offering a valuable service to the team?

- Supporting the support services: Has the programme focused on meeting the needs of the IT teams that will support the new solution?

- Identifying interested parties: Has the eventual owner of the technology been engaged in the programme from the outset?

- Capability development: Has the programme created a capability that can maintain and improve the initial delivery (a capability increment)?

- Realistic benefit estimation: Are benefits realistic and achievable?

- Management of benefit realisation: Are benefits defined and managed at each stage in the lifecycle and are they protected through the use of traceability and oversight by the sponsor?

- Controlling benefit erosion: Has the programme ensured that the product delivered is fit for purpose without substantial workarounds and bugs?

Conclusion

We have looked at ways of working that underpin successful transformation performance, the role of strategy and strategic thinking, how programmes package work up into deliverable chunks, and optimising the delivery of benefits while mitigating risks. Delivery methods, including topics like analysis management and supplier selection, have been discussed. We have also focused on embedding, including the vital role that change management, communications and training play in successful transformation.

Throughout the book I have used examples which I hope will make some of the concepts a little less theoretical and which may align with some of the situations you have experienced or are currently experiencing. If you are embarking on a transformation exercise or you have a transformation programme already in flight and you would like to discuss your specific issues, feel free to reach out to me via LinkedIn.

I wish you all the best with your transformation journey and hope that the checklists at the end of each chapter will provide you with a set of test questions that you can use to explore the health of your inflight programme or that you can apply during programme initiation and delivery, all of which should help you avoid the common causes of failure.

Acknowledgements

I would like to thank all of my colleagues, co-workers and mentors that I have had the opportunity and pleasure to work with and learn from over the past thirty-plus years as a transformation and change agent. They have generously shared their knowledge and expertise with me, and more recently, their real-life personal insights into transformation failures which have helped me to think about the types of situations to cover in this book. It is these experiences and all of the rich inputs that life has offered that have given me the opportunity to learn and grow and made this book possible.

I would also like to thank my beta-readers, in particular Christie Vickers, and of course Lisa Cooper and Helen Lanz from Rethink Press, who improved my material immeasurably.

The Author

 Jane has spent over thirty years working in a wide variety of businesses in operational and change roles where she has directed large teams. She started her career with UPS during a period when the business was rapidly expanding to cover the European market. Jane spent time in the UK leading customer service operations, in Atlanta, US, developing global customer management systems, and in the European regional office setting standards for customer services.

In 1994, Jane joined Legal & General where she held various executive positions associated with operations, change and transformation in the UK. During her time there, Jane spent four years as the Senior Responsible Operator for the establishment of a joint venture insurance business sponsored by the world bank.

In 2015, Jane became an independent consultant helping organisations to improve their end-to-end change capability and deliver large, strategic transformation programmes. Vocal and passionate about all things relating to transformation and change, she loves seeing businesses grow and evolve. Jane is a believer in the saying, 'If you find a job you love, you'll never have to work a day in your life'.

For further information or to contact Jane about specific issues, please reach out to her on LinkedIn:

in www.linkedin.com/in/jelogie